美国高校入学考试指导丛书

SAT 作文

张一冰　编著

上海译文出版社

Contents 目录

第一章　SAT 作文总述

第一节　SAT 作文简介

● SAT 作文是写作的 3 个 section 之一

SAT 考试有 10 个部分（section），其中英文和数学部分各 3 个 section，写作 3 个 section。写作的 section 包括 2 个 section 的语法试题和 1 个 section 的作文。另外还有 1 个 section 的实验题（可以是数学、英文或语法中的任何一种），不计入总分，考生做和不做该 section 对总分没有影响。但考生事先并不知道哪个 section 是实验题，所以，考试时对每个 section 都必须认真对待。

● SAT 的作文得分和语法得分构成了写作的 800 分

SAT 考试的第一个 section 都是作文。这篇要求在 25 分钟内完成的命题作文和另外两个 section 的语法试题，共同构成了写作部分的 800 分。就是说，作文的最后得分会影响写作部分的最后得分。根据每次真题的打分表来看，如果作文满分 12 分，即使 49 道语法试题是 0 分的话，考生依然可以在写作部分的 800 分中拿到 370 分左右。当然，如果 49 道语法试题满分，即使作文 0 分的话，也可以拿到整个写作部分 800 中的 680 分左右。就是说，写作的最后分数要依赖一个考生的语法试题的得分和作文得分的结合（请见第 6 页的 SAT 写作部分打分表。请注意，每次考试的打分表都稍有差别）。

● SAT 作文是由两位阅卷者评判的

一个考生的 SAT 作文将由两位阅卷者评判。阅卷者大部分是美国的中学老师，能迅速看出一个中学生的作文水平。每位阅卷者对一篇作文的给分是从 0 分到 6 分（满分），两个阅卷者所给的分数相加就是该考生的作文得分（从 0 分到 12 分）。但是，如果两个阅卷者对一篇作文的给分相差两分甚至以上，则该篇作文将提交给阅卷委员会评判,以决定该篇作文的最终得分。阅卷委员会的给分为该篇作文的最后得分。比如,一个考生的作文阅卷者 A 给分 4,阅卷者 B 给分 5,则该考生的作文最后得分为 9 分。但是,如果阅卷者 A 给分 4,而阅卷者 B 给分 6,二者相差了两分,则阅卷者 A 和 B 的评分都是无效的,该篇作文将提交给阅卷委员会做最后的评判。

两个阅卷者互相之间可能并不认识,也不知道要对同一篇作文打分,更不知道考生的个人资料。这是为了保证就事论事,就作文本身的质量来打分,避免受到作文本身以外的因素的影响。

一篇作文,如果没有按照命题来写,有可能会得 0 分。当然,考生在答题纸上没有写作,答题纸是空白,该考生的"作文"一定是 0 分。还有个比较严重的情况,要引起我们的重视。有的考生喜欢临时抱佛脚,在正式考试之前背几篇范文,然后生搬硬套到考题上,这实在是个很不聪明的做法。你的范文很难 100％地用到你正式考试时的作文题上,碰到和你背的范文一模一样的考题的机会很小。所以,有时候考生不得不临时对范文进行修修改改,但自己修改的文字和范文的优美文字往往会有很大的出入,这就很容易引起阅卷者的怀疑。更麻烦的是,你背的范文也许别人也背了下来,两个一模一样的作文要是刚好由同一个阅卷者打分,那结果就可想而知了。作文拿个 0 分事小,弄不好还落个学术剽窃的罪名,甚至会左右自己能否去美国深造。所以,再次慎重提醒考生,千万不要一字不动地去背范文。你可以看别人的范文怎么写的,可以广发搜集素材,但正式考试时,你必须要使用自己的语言。

● SAT 作文的答题时间

在所有的美国标准化考试中,SAT 作文的时间最紧迫,只有 25 分钟。在这 25 分钟内,考生要审题、确定思路、组织语言来完成一篇独立的命题作文,可以说,稍微浪费点时间就根本不能有效完成一篇作文。一般来说,审题需要 1 分钟,确定思路及决定论点和论据需要 2 分钟,最后还需要 2 分钟时间对写好的作文通篇阅读校对,以修改一些小错误。所以,真正的写作时间只有 20 分钟。如果考生平时缺乏针对性的训练,要想在那么短的时间内完成一篇作文有很大的挑战。我们建议考生平时多练习在短时间内完成作文的能力,自己给自己规定时间。一开始可以把一篇作文的时间规定在 35 分钟内完成,当你对在 35 分钟内完成一篇作文感到时间上比较能胜任的时候,再把作文时间控制在 30 分钟内,以此类推,逐步适应能在 25 分钟内完成一篇作文。

在考试的时候,作文题上面的东西可以不看,直接看到方框里的东西(作文题都是放在试卷的方框内的），方框外的内容无外乎：你要用铅笔写啊，只能写在划线的答题纸方框内啊，跑题的作文就是0分啊等等。为节约时间，这些考试规则类的东西都要立即跳过，直接看题审题。

● SAT作文的字数要求

对于SAT作文的字数，官方没有给出具体的标准。但从考试的答题纸上可以大概知道考生应该写多少字比较合适。作文的答题纸是两页（见本节后的SAT作文答题纸），共有53行划线。

首先，第一页答题纸一定要写满，写的太少了（比如就写7、8行），会给阅卷者留下很不好的印象，即该考生缺乏想象力，无话可说。一般来说，阅卷者会认为几行字是很难充分论述一个话题的。

其次，对第二页答题纸，如果你认为自己实在无话可说了，又不想犯下太多的语法错误，那么就写满一半或接近一半的篇幅；如果一个考生的语言能力强，想象力丰富，大可把整个第二页写满。能在25分钟内写那么多东西至少从一个侧面证明了自己的写作能力。但是也要注意，你最多只能写两页，千万不要说我写满了，但还没有写完，然后举手问考官再要一张纸。当然，你要了他也不会给你。

对中国学生来讲，要想在25分钟写那么多内容确实有些困难，但又要把第二页写满一半，这时候你可以动点小心思，比如，把字体写得稍微大点，单词和单词之间的间隔稍微大点，起码给阅卷者留个好印象。但是不可以矫枉过正，字体过大或间隔太大都会让人一眼看出你是为了增大篇幅而有意为之，这样反而弄巧成拙。

● 几点要注意的细节

作文答题要用HB以上的铅笔，不能使用钢笔或圆珠笔。

书写要工整、易于辨认，不要使用草体字。我们每个人都认为自己的字体最好认，但事实不是这样的。我们自己应该有这个体会，就是看别人的英文草体会很吃力。同样，你的字体不端正，别人也会很难辨认。说白了，一个阅卷者要是看不懂你的字体，你不能指望他会来回琢磨你那个单词到底是什么。这会在很大程度上影响阅卷者的心情，当然就会进一步影响到你的最后得分。同时，字体不要太小，否则让人看起来很费劲。

切记不要将内容写出方框。因为考生的作文要被扫描到电脑里交给阅卷者评判，而方框外的内容是不会被扫描到电脑里的。很多考生在写作时图方便，一个单词在一行的最后结束不了时，往往就把剩下部分顺手写在方框外了，这在SAT作文考试时候是千万使不得的。

附：SAT 正式考试的作文答题纸

SECTION 1

○ I prefer NOT to grant the College Board the right to use, reproduce, or publish my essay for any purpose beyond the assessment of my writing skills, even though my name will not be used in any way in conjunction with my essay. I understand that I am free to mark this circle with no effect on my score.

IMPORTANT: USE A NO. 2 PENCIL. DO NOT WRITE OUTSIDE THE BORDER!
Words written outside the essay box or written in ink **WILL NOT APPEAR** in the copy sent to be scored, and your score will be affected.

Begin your essay on this page. If you need more space, continue on the next page.

Page 2

Continue on the next page, if necessary.

Continuation of ESSAY Section 1 from previous page. Write below only if you need more space.
IMPORTANT: DO NOT START on this page—if you do, your essay may appear blank and your score may be affected.

Page 3

PLEASE DO NOT WRITE IN THIS AREA

SERIAL #

附：SAT 写作部分打分表

SAT Writing Composite Score Conversion Table

Writing MC Raw Score	Essay Raw Score											
	12	11	10	9	8	7	6	5	4	3	2	0
49	800	800	800	790	770	750	740	720	710	700	680	670
48	800	800	780	760	740	720	710	690	680	670	650	640
47	790	770	760	740	720	700	690	670	660	640	630	620
46	770	750	740	720	700	680	670	650	640	630	610	600
45	760	740	720	710	690	670	650	640	630	610	590	580
44	740	730	710	700	670	660	640	620	610	600	580	570
43	730	720	700	680	660	640	630	610	600	590	570	560
42	720	700	690	670	650	630	620	600	590	570	560	550
41	710	690	680	660	640	620	610	590	580	560	550	540
40	700	680	670	650	630	610	600	580	570	550	540	530
39	690	680	660	640	620	600	590	570	560	550	530	520
38	680	670	650	630	610	600	580	560	550	540	520	510
37	670	660	640	630	610	590	570	550	540	530	510	500
36	660	650	630	620	600	580	560	550	530	520	500	490
35	660	640	620	610	590	570	550	540	530	510	490	480
34	650	630	620	600	580	560	550	530	520	500	490	480
33	640	620	610	590	570	550	540	520	510	490	480	470
32	630	620	600	580	560	540	530	510	500	490	470	460
31	620	610	590	580	550	540	520	500	490	480	460	450
30	610	600	580	570	550	530	510	500	480	470	450	440
29	610	590	570	560	540	520	500	490	480	460	440	430
28	600	580	570	550	530	510	490	480	470	450	440	430
27	590	570	560	540	520	500	490	470	460	440	430	420
26	580	570	550	530	510	490	480	460	450	440	420	410
25	570	560	540	530	500	490	470	450	440	430	410	400
24	560	550	530	520	500	480	460	450	430	420	400	390
23	560	540	520	510	490	470	450	440	430	410	390	380
22	550	530	520	500	480	460	450	430	420	400	390	380
21	540	520	510	490	470	450	440	420	410	390	380	370
20	530	520	500	480	460	440	430	410	400	390	370	360
19	520	510	490	480	460	440	420	410	390	380	360	350
18	520	500	480	470	450	430	410	400	390	370	350	340
17	510	490	480	460	440	420	410	390	380	360	350	340
16	500	490	470	450	430	410	400	380	370	360	340	330
15	490	480	460	450	430	410	390	370	360	350	330	320
14	490	470	450	440	420	400	380	370	360	340	320	310
13	480	460	450	430	410	390	380	360	350	330	320	310
12	470	460	440	420	400	380	370	350	340	330	310	300
11	460	450	430	420	400	380	360	350	330	320	300	290
10	460	440	420	410	390	370	350	340	330	310	290	280
9	450	430	420	400	380	360	350	330	320	300	290	280
8	440	430	410	390	370	350	340	320	310	300	280	270
7	430	420	400	390	360	350	330	310	300	290	270	260
6	420	410	390	380	360	340	320	310	290	280	260	250
5	410	400	380	370	350	330	310	300	280	270	250	240
4	400	390	370	360	340	320	300	290	270	260	240	230
3	390	380	360	350	330	310	290	280	260	250	230	220
2	380	370	350	330	310	290	280	260	250	240	220	210
1	370	350	340	320	300	280	260	250	240	220	210	200
0	350	340	320	300	280	260	250	230	220	210	200	200
−1	330	320	300	290	270	250	230	220	200	200	200	200
−2	310	300	280	270	250	230	210	200	200	200	200	200
−3 and below	310	290	280	260	240	220	210	200	200	200	200	200

第二节　SAT 作文的评分标准及阅卷方式

任何一种考试形式的作文都有其特定的评分标准,SAT 作文也不例外。但评分标准是无法量化的,所以,对一篇作文的最后打分是依赖阅卷者对该作文的总体印象的。

比如,SAT 满分作文的一个标准是逻辑性强,但这个逻辑性强又是怎么量化的呢? 5 分作文的标准是作文具有逻辑性,那么在这一点上,5 分作文和满分作文的逻辑性到底区别在什么地方呢? 达到什么样的标准为逻辑性强呢? 这一切都有赖于阅卷者的主观把握了。

一个阅卷者对一篇作文的评判,无外乎是从内容是否切题、论据是否充分、语言表达是否有效等方面进行的。首先,他会仔细阅读作文的第一段,据此得出该考生的语言能力,然后他会寻找作文的论点是什么,扫描该作文使用的例子是否能充分证明论点,最后,他会浏览作文的结尾,以保证从总体上把握该作文是否完整。一个阅卷者面对那么多的作文,他的时间是非常有限的,据说一篇 TOEFL 作文的阅卷时间大概是 1 分钟,一篇 SAT 作文的阅卷时间最多也就是 2 分钟,考生所要做的就是取悦阅卷者,不断地强化阅卷者对你作文的良好印象,让他在 2 分钟内对自己的作文大加欣赏。

在这里我们先把官方的 SAT 作文评分标准附录如下:

Scoring Guide

SCORE OF 6

An essay in this category demonstrates clear and consistent mastery, although it may have a few minor errors. A typical essay

- effectively and insightfully develops a point of view on the issue and demonstrates outstanding critical thinking, using clearly appropriate examples, reasons, and other evidence to support its position
- is well organized and clearly focused, demonstrating clear coherence and smooth progression of ideas
- exhibits skillful use of language, using a varied, accurate, and apt vocabulary

- demonstrates meaningful variety in sentence structure
- is free of most errors in grammar, usage, and mechanics

SCORE OF 5

An essay in this category demonstrates reasonably consistent mastery, although it will have occasional errors or lapses in quality. A typical essay

- effectively develops a point of view on the issue and demonstrates strong critical thinking, generally using appropriate examples, reasons, and other evidence to support its position
- is well organized and focused, demonstrating coherence and progression of ideas
- exhibits facility in the use of language, using appropriate vocabulary
- demonstrates variety in sentence structure
- is generally free of most errors in grammar, usage, and mechanics

SCORE OF 4

An essay in this category demonstrates adequate mastery, although it will have lapses in quality. A typical essay

- develops a point of view on the issue and demonstrates competent critical thinking, using adequate examples, reasons, and other evidence to support its position
- is generally organized and focused, demonstrating some coherence and progression of ideas
- exhibits adequate but inconsistent facility in the use of language, using generally appropriate vocabulary
- demonstrates some variety in sentence structure
- has some errors in grammar, usage, and mechanics

SCORE OF 3

An essay in this category demonstrates developing mastery, and is marked by ONE OR MORE of the following weaknesses:

- develops a point of view on the issue, demonstrating some critical thinking, but may do so inconsistently or use inadequate examples, reasons, or other evidence to support its position
- is limited in its organization or focus, or may demonstrate some lapses in coherence or progression of ideas
- displays developing facility in the use of language, but sometimes uses weak vocabulary or inappropriate word choice
- lacks variety or demonstrates problems in sentence structure
- contains an accumulation of errors in grammar, usage, and mechanics

SCORE OF 2

An essay in this category demonstrates little mastery, and is flawed by ONE OR MORE of the following weaknesses:

- develops a point of view on the issue that is vague or seriously limited, and demonstrates weak critical thinking, providing inappropriate or insufficient examples, reasons, or other evidence to support its position
- is poorly organized and/or focused, or demonstrates serious problems with coherence or progression of ideas
- displays very little facility in the use of language, using very limited vocabulary or incorrect word choice
- demonstrates frequent problems in sentence structure
- contains errors in grammar, usage, and mechanics so serious that meaning is somewhat obscured

SCORE OF 1

An essay in this category demonstrates very little or no mastery, and is severely flawed by ONE OR MORE of the following weaknesses:

- develops no viable point of view on the issue, or provides little or no evidence to support its position
- is disorganized or unfocused, resulting in a disjointed or incoherent essay
- displays fundamental errors in vocabulary

- demonstrates severe flaws in sentence structure

- contains pervasive errors in grammar, usage, or mechanics that persistently interfere with meaning

Essays not written on the essay assignment will receive a score of zero.

第三节　SAT 作文的出题方式及写作三部曲

下面是 SAT 作文的出题方式。

ESSAY

Time — 25 minutes

The essay gives you an opportunity to show how effectively you can develop and express ideas. You should, therefore, take care to develop your point of view, present your ideas logically and clearly, and use language precisely.

Your essay must be written on the lines provided on your answer sheet — you will receive no other paper on which to write. You will have enough space if you write on every line, avoid wide margins, and keep your handwriting to a reasonable size. Remember that people who are not familiar with your handwriting will read what you write. Try to write or print so that what you are writing is legible to those readers.

Important Reminders：

- A pencil is required for the essay. An essay written in ink will receive a score of zero.
- Do not write your essay in your test book. You will receive credit only for what you write on your answer sheet.
- An off-topic essay will receive a score of zero.
- If your essay does not reflect your original and individual work, your test scores may be canceled.

You have twenty-five minutes to write an essay on the topic assigned below.

Think carefully about the issue presented in the following excerpt and the assignment below.

> Time has a doomsday book, on whose pages he is continually recording illustrious names. But as often as a new name is written there, an old one disappears. Only a few stand in illuminated characters never to be effaced.
>
> *Henry Wadsworth Longfellow*

> **Assignment**：Are there some heroes who will be remembered forever? Or are all heroes doomed to be forgotten one day? Plan and write an essay in which you develop your point of view on this issue. Support your position with reasoning and examples taken from your reading, studies, experience or observations.

正式考试时,考生看到作文考题那一页,和本书上面的形式是一模一样的。我们在前面提到过,为了节约时间,要略过方框以外的内容,因为方框以外的内容每次考试都是一样的,考生应该直接看方框内的作文题。

● SAT 的作文题是由两部分构成的

第一部分叫 Prompt。它往往是带有总结性的几句话,或是从某本书或文章中节选出来的,或是某几句名言。总之,它是个带有提示性的概述,目的是让考生熟悉即将要写的作文主要内容是什么。

第二部分是 Assignment。这才是作文最关键的部分。顾名思义,assignment 就是任务,就是你这篇作文要围绕什么问题来展开。可以说,对 Prompt 的内容你不看都可以,但你必须深刻把握 Assignment 的核心。Assignment 都是问号,考生必须就问题本身来做出正面回答,这个回答就是你的论点,而接下来要举的例子就是你的论据。

● SAT 作文写作三部曲

第一步是审题

对这个题目,我们首先要明白自己到底要回答什么样的问题? 在本题中,问题是:是否有英雄会被永远记住? 或者说,英雄是否注定有一天会被人们遗忘? 本题目可以归纳为是否存在永恒的英雄。

第二步是确定论点

对刚才这个问题,考生要明确自己的观点到底是什么。如果你认为确实有永远的英雄,那么就要举出具体的例子,那个英雄为什么是永恒的;如果你认为没有永恒的英雄,也要举出具体例子,来证明永恒的英雄确实不存在。值得注意的是,对于 SAT 的作文题,你是什么样的观点不会影响你的最后得分,关键是你的观点是否被有效证明。即你的观点并不重要,重要的是你能否找到有效的论据,所以有时候要违背自己的良心。比如这道题,即使你真的认为有永恒的英雄,但如果你的第一反应是有太多的例子可以证明英雄很难永恒，那么，你的论点最好还是写世上没有永恒的英雄。打个比方，即使你认为 Mary 是个很漂亮的女孩子，但你不知道怎么样去具体描写，那么就干脆写 Mary 其实很丑吧（如果你对描写 Mary 很丑有充分把握的话）。在这个问题上不要钻牛角尖，我们写作的目的就是为了拿高分，当然是哪个论点更容易找到事实支持就写哪个论点了，即使你自己也不赞同你的论点。

比如有一篇老托福的作文题，问的是在家吃好还是在外面吃好？哪怕你真的是非常喜欢在外面吃，但是你觉得很难找到 3 个理由来证明在外面吃好，那么就干脆写在家吃好算了，即使你心里并不是这样认为的。对 SAT 作文也是一样，就是在正式确定观点之前，你首先要考虑的是这个观点好不好找例子。事实上，我们的写作三部曲中第二步和第三步是密不可分的。

值得注意的是，SAT 作文的观点，不一定非 A 即 B，你也可以综合二者各自的优势。比如，问 talent 和 motivation 哪个更重要，你不一定非要选其中一个，你的观点也可以是两者都很重要。但是，我们还是建议考生在正式考试时要么选 A，要么选 B，这种写法难度相对小些，而把 A 和 B 综合的写法对写作者的要求自然要高些，弄不好写到最后连自己到底要表达什么观点都弄不清楚了。

一句话，你选个观点不重要，重要的是哪个观点容易找到例子支持。

第三步是确定例子

这点非常重要，可以说是整个写作的核心。你的例子举得好不好，和论点是否密切相关，在很大程度上决定了作文的成败。可以这么说，当我们在做第二步确定论点的时候，事实上是受到第三步影响的。如果发现某个论点更容易找到例子，就确定写该论点。我们从作文要求来看，这个例子可以是从 your reading, studies, experience or observations 中得到的，就是说凡是你能想到的都可以用来作为例子支持你的论点。

这个例子可以是小说里的一个人物，历史上的一个人物或事件，甚至是报纸里报道过的一些人物或事件，也可以是自己亲身经历过的事情等等。关键是该例子和论点是否构成直接有效的关系，是否对论点构成有力的支持。

中式作文喜欢以理服人，英文作文喜欢你讲一个故事来证明一个大道理，所以，举例是整个作文成败之关键。一个学生的阅读量越广泛，他的知识存储越丰富，在举例时候往往就会信手拈来，引经据典，作文的可读性就很强；相反，一个学生如果知识面狭窄，平常不注意积累，到举例时，只能是编几个关于自己的小故事，这样说服力相对就会差很多。所以，为了能举出些有说服力的例子，同学们平时一定要注意作文素材的积累。

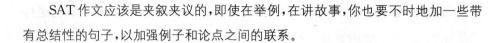

SAT 作文应该是夹叙夹议的，即使在举例，在讲故事，你也要不时地加一些带有总结性的句子，以加强例子和论点之间的联系。

附：该题目的一篇经典范文及点评

Every age, and every culture has its heroes. In some times and places the heroes have been gods or god-like creatures from mythology, or mortals apparently much above the mass of humanity. But today, sports stars, film stars, and political leaders with clay feet have replaced Ram, Achilles, Cleopatra, and Alexander. In fact there are almost no heroes of any age that can withstand our tendency to debunk. There are figures who will always be in the history books, but they won't always be regarded as heroes.

Let's consider Julius Caesar, a hero in his own time but regarded, thanks mainly to Shakespeare's play, as a man with mortal failings: vain, superstitious and arrogant. He can no longer be thought of as a hero, but just a man who came to prominence for his actions at a certain point in history. He has his place in the history of the Western world and his face on ancient coins, but scarcely fits our need for a hero for all times whom we can revere.

Even Shakespeare himself, the writer of immortal plays and poetry cannot fit our need for a heroic figure. He created heroes but cannot qualify as one himself: we know too little about him. History will always try to heap accolades on the man who wrote such sublime words, but that doesn't stop critics from trying to take away his glory. There are those who claim that he didn't even write the plays.

Of course the history books are full of great men and women who are long gone, and no doubt we can all find our personal heroes from their pages. But the dead cannot defend their reputations and so every biography and every film chips away at their greatness. Alexander the Great will never seem so great once we have seen the film.

Finally, we must agree that very few heroes will be revered for all time. The man who saves a child from a tsunami will find himself lauded in the newspapers for a few days, the sports superstars will last a little longer. But no modern human, except for a very few such as Mother Theresa, will be guaranteed a page in the book of all-time heroes.

【点评】

在开始段落,作者首先表明中心论点是这个世界上几乎没有永恒的英雄(there are figures who will always be in the history books,but they won't always be regarded as heroes)。但作者没有急于表达这个中心论点,而是先讲了几句过渡的话,慢慢引到主题上。在第一段,如果作者把下面要举例的两个人(Julius Caesar 和 William Shakespeare)在第一段提及一下会更好。

第二段举了恺撒大帝的例子,他在他那个时代被认为是英雄,但是他有自身性格上的缺陷,这些缺陷拿到现在来看他就不能被称为英雄了,借这个例子,作者说明了没有永恒的英雄。

第三段举了莎士比亚的例子,作者认为莎士比亚虽然创作了许多英雄的形象,但他自己不能被称为英雄,因为我们对他本人还是了解很少的。作者在这里提出了当代文学家一直在争论的一个话题,就是莎士比亚到底是不是那些伟大作品的真正作者。有人认为其实是培根写出那些有争议的作品的,也有人认为是一个写作班子写出那些作品的。从这个例子可以看出作者对文学的涉猎程度。

稍显遗憾的是,两个例子还可以更深刻地挖掘一下,和中心主题之间的联系还可以更紧密些。

第四段是作者的反思,就是历史上有很多英雄的例子,但是后人根据自己的想象不停地对那些英雄事迹进行改写,而死人是无法给自己辩解什么的,所以电影或自传书中的英雄形象多多少少会被人为的东西剥夺光辉,这也是我们为什么很难找到一个真正英雄的原因。

在结束段落,作者再次表明自己的中心观点,即很少有一个所有时代都顶礼膜拜的英雄。同时,为使语气不那么绝对,作者提到了特蕾莎修女,认为很少有人像她那样在任何时代都会被人当做英雄推崇。

总之,这篇作文反映了作者深厚的文学功底和广泛的阅读量,全篇文法正确,思路清晰,并展示了相当水准的遣词造句能力。

第四节 SAT 作文的开头、结尾和正文

我们以下面的一篇 SAT 作文题目作为范本,来详细介绍 SAT 作文的一些写作套路。同时,我们会分析该题目的 6 分、5 分、4 分和 3 分作文之间的不同点。

Think carefully about the issue presented in the following excerpt and the assignment below.

> Intellectuals in America and abroad have debated over the concept of success in American Culture. Success can be defined quite differently by different people, but few people argue that being successful is not considered valuable. However, some people also advocate the view that something considered unsuccessful can also have some value.

Assignment: What is your view of the claim that something unsuccessful can still have some value? Plan and write an essay in which you develop your point of view on this issue. Support your position with reasoning and examples taken from your reading, studies, experience, or observations.

● SAT 作文的开头

任何一篇作文都离不开开头,英文叫 Introduction Paragraph。许多学生对作文的开头感到茫然,他们不知道如何开始一篇文章。作为开始段落,最少要 3 到 5 句话才可以构成一个有效的段落,但许多学生往往一两句就匆匆结束,起码从字数上看就不是个成功的开始段落。

许多学生的一个困惑是,开始段落写什么啊?除了直截了当地回答作文题的问题外,似乎找不到别的内容来充实开始段落。主要原因还是他们没有形成一个开始段落的套路。虽然作文无定论,SAT 作文也没有告诉你应该按照什么方式来开始一个段落,但熟悉套路的好处是,面对一个陌生的题目可以迅速按相关套路组织语言材料,在最短时间内形成一个有效段落。

可以这么说,在开始段落,你必须正面回答作文题的问题。比如,上面这个题

目,问的是你认为人们是否从失败中获得收益?在第一段,这个问题是必须回答的,你的回答可以视作是你这篇作文的中心论点。但许多同学上来就立即回答问题,如有的考生对该题目会这样开始:I think that we can learn something valuable from something unsuccessful。如果这样开始一篇文章,实在过于直接,文章的嚼劲就不足了。如果把中心论点作为一个核心,那么应该有几句过渡的话慢慢绕到这个中心点上,但也不可以绕得太远。

就这个题目,怎样开头呢?

开始段落的基本套路是讲些堂而皇之的话,但是这些话必须要围绕着一些关键词展开。比如本题,问的是是否可以从失败中学到一些有益的东西,那么开头段落就应该围绕着"失败"、"成功"和"学习有益东西"来展开。不妨说点冠冕堂皇的话来充实第一段的内容,然后逐步绕到中心点上,摆明自己的观点。比如可以说,人人渴望成功,但并非人人都可以成功。在成功的路上,失败总是难免的。失败虽然令人不快,让人饱受挫折,但失败是成功之母,只有经历了失败,吸取了更多的教训,才可能获得最后的成功等等。在这个时候可以把自己的观点表明出来了,即我认为人们是可以从失败中获得有益的教训的。你也可以这么开始这篇文章,比如成功的人受到公众的羡慕,有鲜花掌声,金钱地位,但失败的人受到公众的唾弃,甚至是亲人的蔑视等等。这是个鲜明的对比,表明现代社会中成功和失败的两种不同结局。但是,成功的人毕竟是少数。事实上,那些高高在上的成功人士在达到人生的辉煌之前,也经历过许许多多的失败,饱尝过失败的艰辛。但是他们不气馁,而是认真总结失败的教训,并在以后的人生中以此为鉴,避免了许多错误,最终到达成功的彼岸。所以我认为失败是成功的基础,对成功是有帮助的。总之,开头你到底要说什么可以千变万化,但都要围绕几个关键词展开。

在把自己的观点表明后,接下来就该要举例来证明自己的观点了,这个例子可以放在正文里来详细说明,但在第一段还是最好提到下面即将要举的例子,这可以说是全文的 thesis statement。

综上所言,在第一段,你应该表明自己的观点(中心论点),同时要提及将要在正文里列举的例子,在表明中心观点前,讲几句"废话"来慢慢过渡到你的中心论点上。这就是开始段落的套路。

按照这个套路,任何作文题的开始都可以迎刃而解了。在实际操作中,许多学生对中心论点和 thesis statement 都可以很好地把握,关键就是觉得说那几句冠冕堂皇的"废话"很难。其实,说"废话"的能力是可以通过练习慢慢培养的。

任何作文的中心论点就那么一句话,举什么样的例子也是几句话可以讲清楚的,如果考生不具备讲"废话"的能力,整个文章就会显得苍白单薄。

好莱坞巨片泰坦尼克号,让多少观众泪水涟涟。虽然这仅仅是个沉船上发生的爱情故事,但导演的高超导演技巧,让观众一步步走进他的凄美悲凉的世界,四个小时的电影,观众被导演牢牢牵着走,没有丝毫枯燥乏味的感觉。对一个不具备讲废话的导演来说,可能 3 分钟就可以让这个电影结束了。在第一分钟让 Jack 和 Rose 同时登上船并相识,第二分钟让泰坦尼克撞上冰山,第三分钟让 Jack 死掉。但是泰坦尼克在一开始就是很 boring 的,有 30 分钟就在那讲打捞沉船的细节,在观众快不能忍受的时候,导演给 Rose 的眼睛一个大大的特写,从那蔚蓝的眼睛中霎时跳出了泰坦尼克号邮轮,这个经典的爱情故事才算是正式开始了。

这个电影给我们的经典启示就是,一定要学会讲废话,要学会铺垫,把真正激动人心的东西先压抑着,在关键时刻再拿出来。这对 SAT 作文是同样有效的。

● SAT 作文的结束

作文的结尾叫 Conclusion Paragraph。许多同学对怎么样写结尾段落也感到茫然。如同开始段落一样,结尾段落的写法也是有套路可循的。

既然结尾段落是全文的总结,第一句最好把自己的中心论点再重复一次。但是一定要记住,你重复的是你的中心论点,而不是中心论点句子的简单重复。就是说,意思可以是那个中心论点,但句子不能照原来的句子生搬硬套。比如刚才的题目,在第一段作者的中心论点是 value is not only found in success,而在结束段,就最好不要写成 In conclusion, value is not only found in success,这样写太单调了点。可以写成 In conclusion, we can learn something helpful from failures 或者说 In conclusion, failure can teach us something helpful 等等。反正意思不能和中心论点冲突,但在具体的遣词造句上应该灵活点。

许多同学都知道在结束段落首先应该把自己的观点再讲一次,但讲完这个 conclusion 就不知道下面该写什么了,这里也是有套路的。把结论重复后,紧接着就是把自己的论据即刚才的例子再提一下,说明是从这几个例子中证明了刚才的论点的,大致可以写成 From example A and B, we can draw such a conclusion。接下来可以继续发挥下,大致写成 Example A 中的某人或某事没有成功,但他们得到了什么样的教训,从而为什么样的成功打下了基础等等。写到这里,结束段落就算完成一半了。

接下来的一半要写什么呢?好的结束段落往往都会增加些新的内容,要有点画龙点睛的东西,这一点和我们中学里学习作文是一样的。这就要看具体情况怎么样去发挥了。一般来说,如果你认同观点 A 而反对观点 B,在结束段落不妨顺便提一下观点 B 也有可取之处,但切记一句话就够了,免得让阅卷者认为你到文章最后在反驳你自己原来的观点,从而造成立场模糊的感觉。你也可以说观点 A 的正面影响或观点 B 的负面影响,比如刚才的题目,在结束段落的最后一半,可以这么说:如果人们太在意失败,不能从失败中奋起或学到经验,那么,更大的失败往往就是不可避免的。或者说:如果人们只关注成功,就很容易忽视失败给人生带来的正面意义。或者说:虽然人人渴望成功,但那种侥幸的成功是不会长久的,只有经历失败,总结经验教训后获得的成功才是恒久的,等等。总之,就是从文章的论点论据中发点具有积极意义的感慨,让人感觉就这个题目你确实是有感而发。这样,一个完整的结束段落就形成了。

● SAT 作文的正文部分

作文的正文部分(Body Paragraph)是整个文章的核心段落。SAT 并没有明确规定正文到底要写几段,这取决于你到底要举几个例子来支持你的中心论点。如果举一个例子,那正文部分就是一个段落;如果举两个例子,那么正文部分就是两个段落。

我们认为,举两个例子比较合适。如果只举一个例子,对很多中国学生来说,文章恐怕写不长,说服力也不够;要是举太多的例子,限于篇幅,可能每个例子很难写得深刻,同时也显得杂乱。而且,在短时间内要找出更多的例子,对背景知识不是很丰富的学生来讲也会比较困难。所以我们在此建议,正文部分就举两个例子。如果你只举一个例子,你必须对这个例子的内容非常熟悉,有很多内容可写。要对整个例子进行深度挖掘,正文部分往往写成 narrative(叙述)的形式。我们在此提醒各位同学,如果你在考试时实在想不到第二个例子,那就把第一个例子好好发挥吧。

那么到底要怎么样来举例呢?

SAT 命题作文的题目其实是有一定规律可循的。这几年的真题不外乎都是关于名人、成功、失败的教训、人际关系、新技术发展对人类的影响,等等。我们建议考生一定要熟悉一些美国人耳熟能详的名人典故,用以在作文中举例。笔者的一名学生写作功底并不是很强,临考前背了几个例子,自己加以改动发挥,居然都用上了,还拿到了 11 分。这么说不是要学生去背诵,要真那样被阅卷者发现,就彻底完了,不仅会得 0 分,搞不好还会弄出个学术剽窃的麻烦。

尽量不要举中国的例子,你说的东西人家不熟悉,就没有亲切感。比如说恒心的重要性,最好举爱迪生的例子(虽然这个例子已老掉牙了),如果你的例子是愚公移山,或是陈景润多少年如一日研究哥德巴赫猜想,人家根本不知道他们是谁。如果非要举中国的例子,写姚明也好,起码看 NBA 的都知道。准备得越充分拿高分的机会就越大,所谓的一分耕耘,一分收获。

确定了要举的例子之后,就要考虑怎么样去写这个例子了。例子的作用是证明你的观点,不能为了举例而举例。即这个例子和你的中心观点之间的关系要在正文中体现出来,而不能是纯粹在正文部分讲个故事。比如这道题,谈的是失败可以使人们学到有益的东西。所以,例子的侧重点应该放在人们从一个失败的经历中学到了什么东西,而不是一个事情是怎么失败的。这一点请同学们切记。我们接下来会看到该作文题的一个优秀范文,其中举到了哥伦比亚号航天飞机失事的故事,但该范文并没有把主要笔墨放在飞机是怎么失事的,而是美国宇航局从失事中学到了什么东西,对未来的成功有什么正面意义。

上面谈到的关于 SAT 作文的开头结尾和正文的写法,是一个行之有效的套路,同学们可以按这个模式去练习,逐步形成适合自己的一个写作方式。这样,在面对一个作文题时候,就可以做到胸有成竹,下笔有言了。如果没有形成自己的套路,平常不注意练习,在 25 分钟内要想成功组织一篇精彩的文章,恐怕会有很多问题。

根据以上讲解,同学们可以按照这个套路来练习了。每篇练习文章都按照 4 个段落展开,开始段、结尾段加上中间的两个段落(每个例子写一个段落),把 SAT 的四段论文章反复练习,以保证真正考试时候得心应手。

下面是该作文题的几篇考生作文,并逐一附上评析。

SAMPLE ESSAYS WITH SCORES

Think carefully about the issue presented in the following excerpt and the assignment below.

> Intellectuals in America and abroad have debated over the concept of success in American Culture. Success can be defined quite differently by different people, but few people argue that being successful is not considered valuable. However, some people also advocate the view that something considered unsuccessful can also have some value.

Assignment：What is your view of the claim that something unsuccessful can still have some value? Plan and write an essay in which you develop your point of view on this issue. Support your position with reasoning and example taken from your reading, studies, experience, or observation.

6 分作文：（4 段落 2 个例子）

In today's fast-paced, driven society, much emphasis is placed on the final result of an endeavour. American society places a premium on success; our culture has little tolerance for failures or losers. Within this culture framework it sometimes becomes easy to immediately dismiss failures. However, value is not found only in success. As the examples of the recent Columbia shuttle disaster and the Vietnam War demonstrates, events that are not successful still have value.

When the Columbia space shuttle disintegrated upon re-entry, the American people experienced a great tragedy led to a complete investigation of the space program. Deficiencies in the chain of command and the entire culture of NASA were exposed. As a result of the Columbia tragedy, NASA will re-examine its practices and change their ways so something like this doesn't happen again. Surely, this is a valuable thing to come from a horrible failure.

Another unsuccessful endeavour was the Vietnam War. America sent troops to Vietnam to prevent the country from becoming Communist. However, after many years of struggle, the troops were withdrawn and Vietnam fell to the Communist party. But this failure had much value. On one hand, our failure in Vietnam led to an important lesson in successful war strategy. The experience of the fierce guerrilla war led to changes in tactics that later helped America in other conflicts. Also, the Vietnam failure helped change the American culture. People protested the war and the government responded to the voice of the public. These important changes show the value that can come from failure.

Clearly, there is much value in things that are not successful. The Columbia disaster and the Vietnam War are but two examples of unsuccessful events that led to valuable lessons and changes. There is much to be learned from a failure and those who focus only on success will miss out on valuable lessons.

【点评】

这是一篇典型的 4 段落 2 个例子的优秀满分作文。

题目问的是能否从失败中学到有益的东西？作者在第一段讲了几句相关的话后过渡到正题，提出了自己的中心论点即 value is not found only in success。接着，作者用哥伦比亚航天飞机失事和越南战争的例子作为自己的 thesis statement（As the examples of the recent Columbia shuttle disaster and the Vietnam War demonstrates, events that are not successful still have value）。

在第二段,作者首先列举了哥伦比亚航天飞机失事的例子,证明虽然这是个失败,但 NASA 从中学到了许多有益的教训。该段落的重点笔墨不是放在飞机失事的过程,而是放在该失事给 NASA 带来了什么教训。可以说,段落的重点很得当。如果把大量的笔墨耗费在介绍失事过程上,则该段落就是个失败了。另外,在举例结束后,作者把自己的 thesis statement 重复了一下,以加强该例子和中心论点之间的联系(Surely, this is a valuable thing to come from a horrible failure)。

第三段,作者列举了美国越战这一家喻户晓的历史事件,重点提到虽然战争以美国的失败告终,但美国政府从中吸取了经验教训,开始对民众反战的呼声越发重视。在该段落结束的地方,作者也重复了 thesis statement 的内容,但和第二段的重复保持了措辞的区别,虽然核心意思是一回事(These important changes show the value that can come from failure)。

在结束段落,作者先总结了自己的核心观点,并指出以上列举的两个例子可以证明自己的观点,到这里,结尾段落的上半部分就算结束了。紧接着,作者强调,如果只一味强调成功而忽视失败,我们就会漏掉人生中许多宝贵的经验教训。这句话可以说是在对全文做总结,同时又提出了问题的一个反面,和全文呼应。稍显遗憾的是,结尾的后半部分内容有些不足,其实可以再多写一两句,以免给阅卷者留下草草结尾的感觉。总的来说,全文结构清晰,段落自然,文章的笔墨收放自如,作者知道什么地方该渲染,什么地方该一带而过,反映了作者思路清晰,对作文题的把握很准确。另外,对需要重复的地方,作者不是简单地重复原句,而是重复句意,把句子的形式和用词都做了一些改动,以免枯燥。

这篇作文也反映了作者的语言使用技巧和遣词造句能力,如 places a premium on success, dismiss failures, horrific failure 等等。同时,语言非常地道,即使看上去很简单的句子,反映的也是典型的美式思维。

5 分作文:

Success is achievement of something desired, planned, or attempted. However, just because an endeavour was unsuccessful does not mean it is without value. The failed Columbia mission and the Vietnam War are two such examples.

The goal of the Columbia space shuttle mission was to launch safely into space, performing scientific experiments, and to land safely on earth. This was what the crew of and the people at the Houston space centre attempted. This mission was successful until re-entry, when the space shuttle disintegrated without warning. The goal was not achieved; seven astronauts tragically lost their lives. This failure does not mean that this tradgety was without value. It forced NASA to re-examine its contingencies. NASA was compelled to look carefully at its organization structure, independent contractors, and engineering practices. Congress demanded accountability, and was forced to re-examine its budget practices concerning space exploration.

The goal of the Vietnam War was to prevent Communism from taking hold in that country. Many at the time believed that if Vietnam became Communist, so too would the rest of the region. When we left, the country fell to the Communist party. However, advancements in military training came out of the conflict. We learned the value of "special forces" and developed new tactics to fight in environments where tanks were less efficient than air strikes. These lessons better prepared us for modern warfare.

It would be preferable if we did not have to pay such a high price to learn such lessons. The Columbia space tragety and the Vietnam War both demonstrate how events perceived as failures can still have value.

【点评】

这是一篇 5 分作文。

在开始段落，作者提出了核心观点，并且也给出了 thesis statement。所以说，基本的东西都有了，但和 6 分作文开头比较，这篇作文的开头稍显单薄。作者的第一句是对成功的定义，紧接着第二句就说一件事情不成功不代表它没有价值。因此，第一和第二句话之间的过渡显得有点仓促，不是很自然。但不管怎样，开始段落该有的东西还是有了，一个阅卷者想要找的东西在第一段都提到了。

第二段作者介绍了哥伦比亚航天飞机失事的过程及带给 NASA 的经验教训，这个例子确实也能证明作者的中心论点，但是作者没有处理好文章的笔墨，他把大量的文字都用来描写失事带给 NASA 经验教训以外的东西了。起码，该段落的前面两句话是多余的，在这里没有必要介绍哥伦比亚航天飞机的科学任务是什么，没有必要花大量的笔墨在飞机失事之前的东西。同时，该段落结尾处也没有重复 thesis statement 以加强该例子和中心论点之间的联系。

第三段的问题和第二段的问题差不多，还是一个笔墨摆放的问题。

结束段落只有两句话，虽然讲的内容都符合 SAT 作文要求，但只有上半部分，没有下半部分即"发挥"。和开始段落一样，结尾有些仓促，起码应该在此基础上多写两句话。

总的来说，虽然该作文存在一些问题，但由于结构清楚，中心论点明确，举例恰当,符合 SAT 作文的要求,所以拿到了 5 分。另外,作者对语言的把握能力虽然不如 6 分作文作者那样驾轻就熟,但全篇没有什么语法错误,句意也很清楚,即使有点小毛病如拼写错误(tragedy),句式结构还是比较老到的。对一个中学生来说,拥有这样的写作功底也是难得的。

4 分作文:

Some people would say that something that is not successful does not have any value. I would have to disagree with this statement. Sometimes, things that are not successful still have some value. For example, the Columbia space shuttle and the Vietnam War were not successful, but they had value. Thus, it is true that something not successful can still have value.

For instance, the Columbia disaster. Columbia was destroyed in an accident when the shuttle tried to re-enter the atmosphere. This accident was a horrible failure and many people were very upset by it. The value, though, comes from the new way in which we now look at things. Because of Columbia, the space program now know what is wrong. Hopefully, they will change it.

Vietnam is also an example of something not successful. We went to Vietnam in an attempt to get rid of communists. The war went on for a while, but we were not able to win. Many soldiers were killed and the public were very angry about the whole thing. Soon there were many protests across the country and college students especially became active against the war. By the time the war was ended the people were very upset with their country.

These two examples show that something not successful can still have value. As we have seen, both Columbia and the Vietnam War were not successful. Yet, we got something of value out of them.

【点评】

开始段落把中心观点讲出来了,并且也有 thesis statement。但是从第一段就可以看出作者重复性的句子太多了,句式缺少一定的变化。

第二段在介绍哥伦比亚航天飞机失事这个例子的时候,也犯了和 5 分作文相同的错误,就是没有把笔墨的重点放在这件事给 NASA 带来什么教训上,只提到了一句 the space program now know what is wrong,仅仅说他们知道错了,不够具体,应该在此处加上一些具体细节(specific details)。另外,开始一句话是不完整句子(sentence fragment),犯了一个语法大忌。还有就是最后一句(Hopefully, they will change it)显得很勉强,让人感觉作者是无话可说但又想拉长文章篇幅的一个无奈之举,另外使文章的语气有点玩世不恭。

第三段的问题和第二段一样,笔墨分配存在问题。虽就越战本身说了一些不重要的细节,但没有把战争给美国带来什么样的教训说清楚。

最后一段就两句话,显得头重脚轻。

总的来说,这篇作文是个典型的4分作文,作者对作文题有着较深的把握,并且用了适当的例子来证明他的观点,结构清楚,段落自然。但是,由于文章在举例时没有把握好笔墨的重点,导致失分较大。从语法方面看,个别地方外还算通顺,但和满分及5分的作文相比,作者的遣词造句能力和驾驭句式的能力显得很稚嫩。

3分作文:

Sometimes, things that are not successful still have some value. For example, the Columbia space shuttle was not successful but was valuable.

The Columbia disaster it was really sad that the Columbia blew up and the astronauts died. I saw it on my TV and cried. They found pieces for days and days all over Texas. But it was valuable like that Challenger that blew up a long time ago because it makes us want to get it right. We want to fix it so it doesn't happen again and so regular people can go to space like that kid from N * Synch tried to do. And so we will keep going to space and getting satellites for satellite TV and spying and stuff. And so NASA and the President are going to go to Mars next.

Something not successful can still have value because we will go to space even if the Columbia disaster happened.

【点评】

这是一篇让人哭笑不得的跑题作文,能拿3分也足以说明SAT作文给分还是很宽松的。反正笔者教学这么多年,3分的作文我也只见到过一次。

全文只举了哥伦比亚飞机失事的一个例子,没有对该例进行深度挖掘。而且,就是这一个例子,作者也是把笔墨放在介绍失事过程上而不是放在失事给美国带来什么教训上。作者甚至提到了自己痛哭流涕这样具体的无关细节,同时又异想天开说美国总统上火星等等,这些都和文章的主题无关。文章的拼写错误很多,全部都是口语化的东西,虽然SAT没有要求考生把作文写得像academic essay(学术论文)一样,但要是一个阅卷者在批阅一份作文时候,感觉像是在听这个作者面对面地讲话,他能给这个作文很高的评价吗?而且,整个文章的句式死板单调,显得很稚气,不像是个即将进入大学学习的中学生的作品。

从正面来看,作者还是了解了这篇作文的目的,对作文题的要求还是把握住了,有自己的观点,并且知道用例子来支持自己的观点。所以尽管存在这样那样的毛病,阅卷者还是手下留情给了3分。

第五节　叙述形式的 SAT 作文

第三节里,我们介绍了一种 SAT 作文的写作套路,这个套路,仅仅是让同学们在面对一个作文题时候能够迅速组织思路,找到一种写作的捷径,但并不是说每一篇 SAT 作文就必须要这么写。作文无定论,SAT 作文也是一样,只要你的文章能把一个问题说明得深刻而有道理,语言流畅,结构清晰,即使你不按第三节里所介绍的套路写,照样也可以得到高分。

中文的作文喜欢以"理"服人,但西方的惯例是让事实说话,所谓的 Facts are more eloquent than lips(事实胜于雄辩)。对于一个 SAT 作文题,如果你能够讲一个很有说服力的故事,即使不使用第三节介绍的套路,而使用纯粹叙述形式(narrative)的写作方式,也不失为一种有效的写作。

但是要记住,即使使用叙述形式的写作方式,开头段落还是应该包括中心观点和说明性的句子。

使用叙述形式的写作方式,往往都是说一个故事,即用 one example 的形式,而在讲故事时候要侧重于故事本身的生动性,可以不考虑 thesis statement 的重复等问题。你的任务就是讲故事,不要被第三节所介绍的一些条条框框所影响。

在决定写叙述形式的作文时,考生要切记,你这个故事一定要有足够的长度,故事的本身要有一定的吸引力,能够很好地说明论点。这对考生语言能力的要求很高。没有足够的语言能力,很难写到一定的篇幅,这样文章的说服性就不够。同时,你对这个故事要有足够的了解,要真的觉得有东西可写。这个故事,可以是你自己的故事,也可以是你周围人的故事,也可以是文学作品或是历史中的一个故事。总之,这个例子本身确实能打动人,要不落俗套。

比如,在第三节里那个关于是否从失败中学到有益经验的作文题,笔者有许多学生会写自己新到一个陌生的国家,语言能力弱,然后写自己怎么样克服语言障碍,这其中写参加什么语言考试失败,然后是如何从失败中获得教训,最后是怎么成功的故事。这个故事本身太不新颖了,很难打动阅卷者。

在那篇关于哥伦比亚失事的范文里,如果你对这个事情本身比较清楚,你完全可以把哥伦比亚失事这件事写成个 narrative 的形式,甚至花点笔墨来描写失事的过程都无伤大雅。但是,文章的核心还是要侧重于在失事后美国有关方面是怎么样处理这件事的,怎么样进行深刻反思的,做了哪些事来检讨自己的工作,从中得到了什么样的教训等等。对于越南战争的例子,重点部分依然要落实到美国军方和政府对此事的反思,它对美国调整其战争策略起到了什么样的作用等。当然,这对考生的知识结构要求就很高了,考生没有足够的知识面,对例子本身缺少了解,是很难写到一定的长度的。

下面我们介绍一篇获得满分的叙述形式的文章:

Think carefully about the issue presented in the following excerpt and the assignment below.

No one is contented in this world, I believe. There is always something left to desire, and the last thing longed for always seems the most necessary to happiness.

— Marie Corelli, *A Romance of Two Worlds*

Assignment：Do you think that people are capable of finding happiness or are they always searching for something beyond what they have? Plan and write an essay in which you develop your point of view on this issue. Support your position with reasoning and example taken from your reading, studies, experience, or observation.

优秀范文：

Happiness means different things to different people. My sister is happiest when she performs onstage in a play. My best friend is happiest when he is pitching a perfect game on the baseball field. People find happiness in all sorts of ways, but that doesn't mean they stop searching for something more. Finding happiness and continuing to pursue other goals are not mutually exclusive propositions. Instead, both of these activities can work together to motivate you, as I've learned from my own experience.

When I was in middle school, my favourite class was art and I was disappointed that the class period was so short and only twice a week. Although I was happy during those times, I really missed art during the rest of the week. However, knowing that art class was approaching helped motivate me to pay attention in the rest of my classes because I knew that my "reward" would soon follow. Once we were in the art room and I was immersed in painting or sculpting or drawing, I found incredible happiness in the creative process and carried this feeling with me throughout the remainder of the day, yet I wasn't fully satisfied with this small amount of exposure and I wanted more. I did appreciate the happiness I had, but at the same time I was looking something beyond that.

So I begged my parents to let me take art classes after school and on the weekend, I managed to convince them I'd be happier if I could have this additional creative time. Taking more and different art classes outside of school exposed me to a variety of different techniques and media that I never had time to explore in school, like metal-working, wood-carving and print-making. I grew even more enthusiastic about the visual arts and found even more happiness than I could have imagined thanks to these additional classes. By wanting something more, I was able to find additional contentment and inspiration and I truly was happy with the results.

Yet I didn't stop reaching for other goals. I really wanted to have my artwork displayed for the public, so I worked very hard for several years to develop a portfolio and I achieved my goal last year with my first solo show at a local gallery. This success gave me much happiness, and I'm already planning additional shows. Being content with my art makes me happy on a regular basis, but this doesn't keep me from wanting something more at the same time. For me, striving for additional goals adds to my happiness, so I don't see the two actions as contradictory at all. Instead, searching for something beyond what you have can help you to appreciate and enhance whatever it is that makes you truly happy.

【点评】

这个作文题问的是，人们能否寻找到快乐，或人们是否总不满足于眼前的快乐？

在第一段，作者首先说明对不同的人来说，快乐意味着不同的内容，人们可以找到快乐，但不会就此停止。接着作者说自己的经历能证明人们可以找到快乐并在此基础上继续寻找更大的快乐。在第一段，作者并没有直接点题，而是说了几句"废话"来逐步过渡到自己的中心论点上。

第二段提到了自己在中学时代的艺术课上得到许多快乐，在第二段的最后，作者说因为艺术课的课时太少，感到很不满足。

第三段提到了为了追求更大的满足，作者在周末参加艺术课程的训练班。在第三段最后一句，作者提到从中获得了更大的快乐。

在第四段，作者笔锋一转，再次提到即使参加艺术训练班也不能满足了，他要把自己的作品展示出来,并且终于成功地举办了自己的个人画展。在全文结束,作者提到,追寻更大的快乐可以让自己更珍惜眼前的快乐,并使这样的快乐程度更强。

综合全文看,作者以自己在艺术道路上的成长经历来证明一个道理,即人们可以从眼前的事情中找到快乐,但却不会满足。总体而言,该文采用 narrative 的方式,但是在开始段和结尾,作者采用的是议论方式,阐述自己的观点。文章虽然以 narrative 方式为主,但也不纯粹是在讲故事,而是用适当的笔墨把这个故事揭示的含意和 assignment 联系。用一个例子进行发挥,介绍了自己三个阶段的快乐,层层递进。这充分说明作者对 prompt 和 assignment 进行了深刻的审题,进而深刻了解作文的要求。

另外,作者在适当的时候用了一些过渡词(如 although,however,yet,but,instead 和 so 等),使文章的逻辑性更加清晰。如在第二段的最后一句使用 yet 开始,表示自己不满足于眼前的快乐,而在第三段使用 so 开始,和第二段构成了呼应,段落之间的过渡因为这些过渡词而显得十分自然。

最后,作者的语法基础很扎实,通篇没有语法错误(当然,即使有点小的语法错误也不会影响该篇作文获得满分),而且展示了一定的遣词造句能力。如第一段的 mutually exclusive propositions,第二段的 incredible happiness、small amount of exposure 等等。另外,文章的句式结构灵活,是简单句和复杂句的混合,该简单就简单,该复杂就复杂,同时复杂句里把句子的核心内容用主句形式表达,次要内容用从句形式表达,如第一段最后一句 Instead,both of these activities can work together to motivate you,as I've learned from my own experience。这一句里,作者把核心内容先用主句形式写出来,接着用连词 as 引导一个从句说明自己的经历可以证明主句的内容。

第二章　SAT 满分作文点评

　　收集在本章的 10 篇优秀范文,都是 SAT 满分作文的典范之作,其中第 9 和第 10 篇系笔者的学生最近参加 SAT 考试的满分作品,笔者一字未改,只是为了让同学们一窥 SAT 满分作文的真实面貌。

　　这些满分作文,尽管每一篇都存在这样那样的小缺憾,但这些小缺憾相对于整篇文章来说无异白璧微瑕,它们并不影响该篇文章整体上的优秀。这些作者,在深刻把握写作要求的基础上,能够鲜明地表达自己的观点,都能够选择非常具有说服力的例子来证明自己的观点。作者的思路清晰,逻辑严密,让阅卷者充分相信,该作者确实是深刻理解了题目的要求,非常清楚他要做什么,而且知道怎么样来做。

　　这些作文有的使用一个例子,有的使用两个甚至更多的例子。使用一个例子的作文,能把这一个例子进行充分挖掘,建立例子和主题之间的紧密联系。同时,这些作文有的以叙述见长,有的以说理见长,但都显示了作者缜密的思维和令人信服的说理方式。

　　在语言风格上,有的作文用词比较简单,但句式结构多变,语言地道,符合英文的表达习惯;有的作文用词相对典雅,但恰到好处,并无炫耀词汇量之嫌,而且用词和整篇文章的风格也很吻合。从字数上来看,所有的满分作文都达到了一定的量,让阅卷者认为作者确实有话要说,思想深刻。

　　最后,从满分作文中的例子的内容来看,涉及人文、历史、文学和科学等方方面面的内容,这些作者充分展示了自己广泛的阅读量,对不同领域的涉猎,这无疑都会给阅卷者留下深刻的印象。我们一再强调,同学们一定要广泛阅读,广泛收集各类经典素材,以备写作举例时使用的一个重要原因。

　　希望同学们仔细阅读欣赏这 10 篇经典范文,从中学习它们的长处,对照自己的习作,找到自己的短处,在今后的 SAT 写作中不断提高自己的写作技巧和水平,力争考试时获得 5 分以上的成绩。

范文一 人的价值取决于其创造的 数量还是质量

Think carefully about the issue presented in the following excerpt and the assignment below:

> In a society hat judges self-worth on productivity, it is no wonder we fall prey to the misconception that the more we do, the more we're worth.
>
> —— Ellen Sue Stern, *The Indispensable Woman*, 1988

Assignment: what do you think of the idea that a person's worth is based on how much he or she produces? Is this an accurate scale for measuring worth or should we use different criteria to make this judgement? Plan and write an essay in which you develop your point of view on this issue. Support your position with reasoning and examples taken from your reading, studies, experience, or observation.

6 分范文:

The debate about quality versus quantity occurs in a variety of settings: Is twenty pages better than ten for a term paper? Is an all-you-can-eat buffet preferable to a gourmet meal? Is a huge lawn more desirable than a small yard? As a society, we tend to value the quantity of productivity to determine how successful a person is. Focusing on the amount produced, however, is based on the false assumption that quantity by itself is an appropriate judge of worth. In fact, the quality of a product is far more important, as we can see by looking at examples from current events and literature.

One of the biggest recent scandals in the business world involved many executives from Enron. These men were focused on how much they could produce, on how much money they could make for themselves. To increase their production, they engaged in risky, illegal, and unethical business practices that eventually led to the total destruction of the entire company and ruined the lives thousands of Enron employees and investors. Although the dollar value of these men may have been very high at one time, their current value and worth has plummeted. If we think of value in another sense, with a humanitarian or social slant, it becomes even more obvious that these men now have little worth in the eyes of their peers, former employees, and former stockholders. The Enron executives should have focused on making a quality product rather than on quantity in order to maintain a successful company along with satisfied employees and stockholders.

In the literary world, success is measured by the number of books sold. Authors who sell millions of books are valued more than those who sell hundreds of books, so it appears that worth, in this case, is best judged by a writer's productivity. This scenario, however, is misleading, since one writer may produce a single work that becomes a best-seller in comparison to another writer who produces dozens of works each of which sell a limited number. Which writer truly has more worth? A specific example o illustrate this scenario is Bill Clinton compared to Judy Blume. Clinton recently published his memories, which will likely be very successful and become a best-seller. Blume, the author of many books for teenagers, probably hasn't and won't ever appear on the best-seller list. Is Clinton worth more because his name and political career make his book successful? Or is Blume worth more because her portrayals of teen life affect many meaningful criteria of judging worth.

Each person's idea of self-worth is based on many factors, including productivity. If we focus on this particular standard for evaluating worth, however, we lose sight of fact that quality is just as important as — if not more than — quantity. For this reason, we should not cling to the false belief that the more we do, the more we worth.

【作者观点分析】

本文能得满分,开头的第一句话起到了很大的作用。因为它用 The debate about quality versus quantity 就总结出了题目中没有出现的却暗含的争辩——"质量和数量,哪个更重要?"

衡量一个人价值的标准是什么? 如果我们认定 a person's worth is based on how much he or she produces,那么我们就会得到这样的结论: the more we do, the more we're worth;而对于这样的态度,我们考生知道,应该是反对的,因为有 fall prey to the misconception 这类的字眼提示,我们应该寻找另外的标准。本文作者

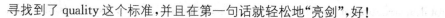

寻找到了 quality 这个标准，并且在第一句话就轻松地"亮剑"，好！

【文章内容分析】

作者的开头使用了一系列反问句，值得我们学习。在讲了几句相关的提示性话语后，作者非常鲜明地提出了自己对这个问题的看法（In fact，the quality of a product is far more important），并接着通过写最近发生的例子及文学界的一些例子来支持自己的观点。

在第二段，作者举了美国安然公司的丑闻事件，指出公司高层只顾拼命生产而忽视质量，最终导致公司破产。所以作者认为在许多人看来，尽管这些高层的 dollar value 曾经很显赫，但在同行和雇员看来，他们是没有价值的。

第三段，作者举了美国前总统克林顿和美国儿童小说作家 Judy Blume 的例子，但作者没有把他们两人的价值进行比较，这个比较留给了读者。在文学界，一般会认为一个作者书卖得越多，他的价值越大，但作者提出了一个发人深思的问题：克林顿的传记因为自己的政治名声而登上畅销书宝座，传记的销量惊人，而 Blume 虽然没有克林顿的名气，但她创作了大量的儿童故事书，影响了一代又一代的美国人；虽然她所有书的销量还赶不上克林顿一本书，但你能就此认为她的价值就不如克林顿吗？作者的态度不言自明。

在结束段，作者提到，一个人的价值取决于许多方面，而不仅仅是他的productivity，并且指出了 the more we do，the more we're worth 这句话其实是错误的。

【写作语言分析】

全篇结构严密，举例非常恰当，充分证明了人的价值不仅仅取决于他的创造量。两个例子一个是曾鼓噪一时的美国安然事件，一个是美国前总统和一个儿童故事书作家的对比，都是阅卷者耳熟能详的。并且文章使用了一些过渡词，如 one of，although，however，a specific example，for this reason 等，使得全文逻辑严密自然。全篇没有语法错误和拼写错误，说明作者留下了足够的时间去校对自己的文章，使阅卷者对该文的良好印象进一步加深。

范文二　动力和天分哪个更重要

Think carefully about the issue presented in the following excerpt and the assignment below:

> "Champions aren't made in gyms. Champions are made from something they have deep inside them: A desire, a dream, a vision. They have to have last-minute stamina, they have to be a little faster, they have to have the skill and the will. But the will must be stronger than the skill."
>
> — By Muhammad Ali

Assignment: If you want to become an expert in a certain field, do you need to have more alent or more motivation? Plan and write an essay in which you develop your point of view on this issue. Support your position with reasoning and examples taken from your reading, studies, experience, or observation.

6 分范文:

To me, being an expert means being successful, and achieving success requires lots of hard work, time, and practice. This is true regardless of what you pursue, from running to drawing, acting to skating, teaching to dancing. Yet expertise and success don't come from skill alone. To truly succeed, you need to have at least as much motivation as talent, because if you don't posses the desire to do something, your talent may simply wither from neglect, and people who prove this to be the case include Jewel and my sister.

Pop singer Jewel has a critically acclaimed voice and songwriting skills. She's won awards for her songs and succeeded in the music business. Yet she didn't achieve fame and fortune simply with her talent. Instead, she struggled and worked incredibly hard for many years before she ever found success. In fact, at one point she was living in her car because she didn't have enough money to support herself, but she never gave up or stopped believing in her dream to play guitar and sing.

Jewel's strong motivation and drive finally paid off when she was "discovered" by a music producer and her recorded albums showed off her talent and sold well to the general public, making her a successful expert in her field.

My sister is a contrast to Jewel's effective combination of talent and motivation. When she was little, my sister showed natural talent as a dancer, and my parents enrolled her in classes to develop her talent. My sister, however, didn't care about dancing, so she never practiced or put any effort into her classes. Eventually, my parents realized that they were wasting their money to pay for the training because even though she had talent, my sister's lack of will meant that her talent became useless, because she needed to work to transform her talent into true skill and experience in order to achieve success, but she didn't have the motivation to follow through with this.

By looking at the contrasting examples of Jewel and my sister, both with natural talent but only one with the matching will to succeed, you can see that motivation is the critical factor for success or expertise in a field. You can only really make full use of your talent if you have the will to succeed.

【作者观点分析】

本文的题眼在于："是 motivation 重要还是 talent 重要"？作者的态度是"To truly succeed, you need to have at least as much motivation as talent"。接着，作者进一步说明，talent 离开了 motivation 就会凋谢枯萎。

从拳王阿里的引言中，我们看到比较倾向性的观点，阿里所说的"will"和"skill"，其实就是题目中所讲到的"motivation"和"talent"。阿里的态度是"But the will must be stronger than the skill"（意志力必须强过技巧，才可能成为冠军）。那么，我们可以认定，选择 motivation 更安全。（当然，到底如何写，考生可以有不同的见解，只要说得合理就行。）

【文章内容分析】

在开始段，作者提出自己的观点，如果只有 talent 而没有 motivation，要想获得成功是不可能的（To truly succeed, you need to have at least as much motivation as talent, because if you don't posses the desire to do something, your talent may simply wither from neglect）。接着，作者提到将要讲到的两个例子，一个是美国歌手 Jewel 的故事，一个是他妹妹的故事。作者在提到自己的观点前，也讲了一些"废话"来丰富第一段的内容。

第二段，作者提到 Jewel 曾经非常落魄，还举了一些细节比如她一度以自己的车子为家（she was living in her car），但是她坚信自己成为一代歌手的梦想会实现。

正是在这个梦想支持下，她度过了生命中最艰难的时刻，最后被一个音乐制作人慧眼识珠，出版了她的唱片从而获得了成功。这个例子证明 Jewel 有 talent（a critically acclaimed voice and songwriting skills），但更重要的是她有 motivation，所以她才获得了成功。

第三段，作者举她的妹妹为例。妹妹自幼具有舞蹈天分，所以家里人把她送到舞蹈学校进行专业训练，但是妹妹缺少动力（My sister, however, didn't care about dancing, so she never practiced or put any effort into her class），所以最终家里人也放弃了梦想。作者在最后提到，妹妹虽然天分很好，但缺少动力，因而这样的天分没有被好好利用，所以没有在舞蹈上取得成功。

在结束段，作者提到天分只有和动力结合，才能创造出成功的奇迹，把自己的观点再次重申了一次。

全文的开头和结尾都非常符合 SAT 作文的要求，特别是两个例子构成了鲜明的对比，对支持作者的观点起到了非常正面的作用。这篇文章也提醒了我们，尽量举出一些带有对比性质的例子，从而增加文章的说服力，因为是好是坏，是对是错，一对比就看得清清楚楚了。

【写作语言分析】

文章结构清楚，段落过渡自然（如第三段的第一句话起到了承上启下的作用，即 My sister is a contrast to Jewel's effective combination of talent and motivation.）。作者具有一定的驾驭语言的能力（如 wither from neglect 等），句式结构多变，该简单就简单，该用笔墨的地方就用笔墨，而且全文没有文法上的错误。文章也使用了一些转折词，使文章自然流畅（如第二段的 yet, instead, but，第三段的 however, but, eventually 等）。

范文三　事情的本身还是对事情的
态度决定了你的快乐

Think carefully about the issue presented in the following excerpt and the assignment below：

> "I am more and more convinced that our happiness or unhappiness depends far more on the way we meet the events of life, than on the nature of those events themselves"
>
> — Wihelm von Humboldt

Assignment：Which do you think contributes more to personal happiness： what happens to you or the way you respond to what happens? Plan and write an essay in which you develop your point of view on this issue. Support your position with reasoning and examples taken from your reading, studies, experience, or observation.

6分范文：

There's a common saying usually applied to sports："It's not whether you win or lose, it's how you play the game. " This saying, however, can easily be applied to how we live and whether or not we are able to achieve personal happiness. As the Humboldt quotation suggests, it's not the events that occurs in our lives but rather the way we react to these events that most affects our happiness. Excellent representations of this can be found in Shakespeare's "Hamlet," where characters respond differently to the same situation and gain varying levels of happiness because of their respective reactions.

Gertrude, for example, responds to the death of her husband, the King, by remarrying shortly after his death. Rather than dwelling on her new role as widow and the accompanying sorrow and misfortune that have fallen upon her, she chooses to react by quickly recovering and aligning herself with her former brother-in-law. Given her situation, this is a very intelligent and rational decision, for it provides her with the security of a strong marriage as well as a continued high status as queen, since Claudius has now ascended to the throne. Gertrude positively responds to a negative event rather than letting that event destroy her.

In contrast, Hamlet reacts to his father's death by obsessing about what happened and by brooding over his mother's remarriage. Because of his vision of the ghost, Hamlet begins o believe that his father was murdered, but instead of acting decisively on this information and confronting his uncle directly, Hamlet ponders his vision and sinks deeper and deeper into his sorrow and depression. Allowing himself to be heavily influenced by everything that is happening around him, Hamlet eventually succumbs to his despair and dies along with several other characters in the final scene of the play. Hamlet is a prime example of someone who lets happiness be ruled by outside forces rather than choosing how to react to events to exert some control over his own emotional stale of mind.

Although Gertrude and Hamlet are fictional characters, the way Shakespeare portrays them is representative of real human behavior. Many people let themselves be influenced by what happens to them, like Hamlet, and these people have difficulty finding happiness. On the other hand, some people, like Gertrude, react in a more positive way to any event that occurs and thus achieve a certain level of personal happiness regardless of what happens. This contrast proves that our reaction to events rather than the events themselves is the critical factor for achieving happiness.

【作者观点分析】

德国近代著名的自由主义政治思想家、教育家、外交家、比较语言学家和语言哲学家威廉·冯·洪堡(Wihelm von Humboldt,1767—1835),倡导"学术自由"和"教学与研究相统一"的精神。他的名言可翻译为:

"我对此越来越深信不疑——人的快乐还是不快乐,不取决于事物本身,而取决于对事物的态度。"

整句话比较的是"态度"与"事物"对于人的影响力。很明显,洪堡倾向于唯心的"态度"。因此,作者也顺着洪堡的思路,支持"态度"更加重要的观点。

【文章内容分析】

作者通篇使用的是"哈姆雷特"中的两个人物——丧夫后迅速结婚的王后Gertrude,以及悲剧色彩凝重的王子 Hamlet。两个人物,黑白对比,各占满满一段,其篇幅之重,使得文章更像是一篇文学论文,而论述的视角也不同于平时的 common sense。

我们一般看到的评论是,王后不应该在丈夫尸骨未寒时马上再嫁,王子为父报仇,虽然最后自己也死了,但勇气可嘉云云。而本文说王后寻找到了人生的快乐,而王子无法自拔于丧父悲伤,最终为抑郁所害。这观点读起来新奇有余,几乎令读者目瞪口呆。但是,这也从另外一个角度说明了作者思维独特,不愿人云亦云。这种思辨特质也是美国名校所青睐的,本文获得高分也就不足为奇了。(不怕犯错,不怕好笑,就怕没有独到的见解,这种特点,与我们中国学生比较循规蹈矩的习惯并不符合。所以大家在组织观点时,一定要注意规避中式英语及中式思维。)

【写作语言分析】

下面我们再从写作的语言角度看看本文还有哪些可圈可点之处。

文章引用运动场上的一句常用语 It's not whether you win or lose, it's how you play the game. (结果不重要,过程重要)。这与洪堡的名言"事物不重要,态度重要"有异曲同工之妙。

注意! 这里使用了一个非常高明的 restate(复述)技巧。文章开端时,往往需要对题目的观点进行 restate,大家在做这个必要功课时,一定要避免重抄,而应该是改写,或者用自己的语言复述,更好的是用另一句名言进行论证。

本文作者在句子结构方面的驾驭能力,可以从以下几个例子看出一二。

<u>As the Humboldt quotation suggests</u>, it's not the events that occurs in our lives but rather the way we react to these events that most affects our happiness.

Gertrude, <u>for example</u>, responds to the death of her husband, the King, by remarrying shortly after his death.

Many people let themselves be influenced by what happens to them, <u>like Hamlet</u>, and these people have difficulty finding happiness.

<u>Given her situation</u>, this is a very intelligent and rational decision, for it provides her with ...

第一个句子划线部分是状语从句,放在句首表原因;

第二个句子划线部分是插入语,表附加细节;

第三个句子划线部分是插入语,表附加细节;

第四个句子划线部分是独立结构中的分词结构,放在句首表原因。

在写长句子时,作者倾向于使用从句,独立结构,插入语进行句子的变化。

我们在前面分析过如何变化用词,变化用句;尽管都是"变化",但用词变化需要努力扩大词汇量，只要留意，就可以达到"四两拨千斤"的效果。

　　句子结构的变化一个非常大的优点，就是文章长短交叉，错落有致。相对于简单句子的罗列、并列句的啰嗦，从句和独立结构有自己独到的优点。

范文四 我们真的希望听到别人真心的建议吗

Think carefully about the issue presented in the following excerpt and the assignment below:

> Former Secretary of State Colin Powell has stated: "Loyalty means giving me your honest opinion, whether you think I'll like it or not."

Assignment: Do you agree or disagree that people *really* want others to give them their honest opinion? Plan and write an essay in which you develop your point of view on this issue. Support your position with reasoning and examples taken from your reading, studies, experience, or observation.

6分范文：

Most people in the world, if asked, will say that they want an honest opinion from their friends and coworkers. Is this really true? There are many things people do or say in their everyday lives that contradict this supposed desire for honesty.

The thing that most people are guilty of is asking a question and expecting a specific response. For example, if I wrote this paper and asked my teacher if it was any good, I might expect her to say yes. Not necessarily because it really is a good paper, but because I don't want to get my feelings hurt if she tells me no. Why, then, do people ask these questions? To receive some sort of encouragement, regardless of whether it is an honest response or not.

Perhaps another thing that gives this away is the asking of a question that cannot be answered correctly. One of the most popular examples of this is when a woman asks someone if she looks fat in whatever she is wearing. It may seem like a simple, harmless question, but there is, in fact, no right way to answer this question. If the reply is yes, the woman will surely get angry and upset because now she thinks she's fat. However, if the reply is no, she will surely accuse the responder of lying. In situations like these, it may be best to just not answer at all.

I know that's my father's philosophy when my mother poses such questions.

In these instances such as these, more people show that they in fact do not want honest opinions, but to hear what they want to hear. However, this does not mean that they are not loyal friends or that they do not have loyal friends. A loyal friend will probably tell you the truth when you need to hear it. But what is perhaps more important to many people is that a loyal friend also knows just how and when to lie.

【作者观点分析】

美国前国务卿鲍威尔,作为美国历史上第一个黑人国务卿,"和为贵"是他信奉的宗旨,通常被人们视为比较典型的"鸽派"人物。他的这句名言,可翻译为:对于"忠诚"的定义,是给出"真实"的想法,而不在意对方的"倾向性"。

关于"argumentation"与"report"

有一点大家必须非常注意:

鲍威尔这句话的核心,不是忠诚是什么,而是讨论"真实"还是"照顾对方的情绪"两者的倾向问题。鲍威尔的态度是"真实"优先。(倘若我们去讨论"忠诚是什么",那就跑题了!)

我们在任何写作开始,就必须确定,这篇文章是 argumentation(议论)还是 report(报告)。一般而言,SAT 以 argumentation 为多。因此,文章结构是四段式,开头一段把题目意思用其他语言摆一摆,当前局势点一点;第二段说正面,必须使用例证进行支撑;第三段说反面,该段最后一个句子要说,这个其实不影响事物本质云云;最后一段再把作者的意见重新提出一次。这样文章看起来就比较平衡,又不失自己的见解。

倘若是 report,就不需要两面都讲了,文章结构一般采用五段式:开头一段还是和 argumentation 类似;在第二、三、四段,要把一个事情分成三个层次,详细讲述;结尾再重复一下观点。

这是非常常见的套路,相信大家也运用得比较顺心应手了。从 assignment 中"Do you agree or disagree"我们就能看出,这是要我们给观点的。我们可以使用四段式进行常规作文。但是在实战中,有时候不说反面,第二、三段都说正面,也有令人惊喜的地方——那就是,攻击力集中,说服力大大增强。本文就是一例。

【文章内容分析】

文章的开头有三句话,有各自不同的功能,真正做到了"短小精悍"。第一句,摆现实(暗含作者不支持的观点);第二句,有力地反问(Is this really true? 我们在前面第一篇文章的分析中也提到过反问句的威力,希望大家尝试使用。但"把戏不可久玩",这种反问句在一篇文章中使用频度不宜过高。一次反问,一串反问都行,就是不要到处都是疑问);第三句话,明确作者的观点:There are many things people do or say in their everyday lives that contradict this supposed desire for honesty(生活中有很多人们并不追求真实的例子)。

文章的第二段和第三段,作者显然是对语言学中的委婉语现象有一定的了解,或者说阅读过相关文章,因此有两个非常有趣的例子进行说明。

委婉语 euphemism 一词源自希腊语的前缀 eu＝well 和词根 pheme＝speaking。委婉语是人类使用语言过程中的一种普遍现象,它不仅是一种社会语言现象,更是一种文化现象。委婉语的一个功能是在交际中避免冒昧和非礼,当迫不得已要涉及令人不快的事情时,应选择委婉的表达法以避免伤害对方的感情。

第二、三段提到的就是两例典型的委婉语现象。第二段举的例是说,人们有时候问问题不是为了"是与否",而是直奔"是"而去,对这样的提问,聪明的听众只会送"是"。比如:我的论文写得怎样啊?(问话的肯定是想听表扬才问啊!)

第三段是有些问题属于"两难问题",无法回答"是与否";对这样的提问,聪明的听众往往会沉默,此时无声胜有声。比如:妻子问丈夫"我美不美?"(说美吧,不是事实,说了也被怀疑拍马屁;说不美吧,又怕被打,只好沉默了)

这两段文字幽默,但又决不重合现象,因此,非常具有杀伤力。尤其是第三段结尾的一句"I know that's my father's philosophy when my mother poses such questions."用了两个书面语的大词"philosophy"与"poses questions",自揭家里的小小尴尬,把阅卷的考官一下子逗笑,高分也就志在必得了。

结尾段,牵涉到一个非常重要的论证方法:证实与证反。

从提问中"Do you agree or disagree that people *really* want others to give them their honest opinion?",我们不难发现有一个斜体的"really"。

这就暗示我们,本题可以考虑使用证反题的方式来反驳。

证明可以分为"证明某事是真的"以及"证明某事为假的"两大类。其中,后者比较简单,为什么呢? 因为只要列举一个反例就行了。比如说:"中国南方没有美女"这个命题,只要能找出某人是美女,而她正好是南方人,那么这个命题就破了。

本文的第二、三段都是证明了"在 XX 情况下,有的人说话并不是为了要对方告知事实"的存在,因此属于典型的证反文章。

对于这样的文章,结尾段要非常注意,因为一味证反,会让人觉得过于咄咄逼人,因此往往在最后一段进行平衡。"A loyal friend will probably tell you the truth when you need to hear it. But what is perhaps more important to many people is that a loyal friend also knows just how and when to lie."文章结尾的两个句子,虽然

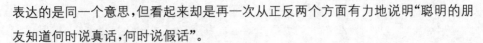

表达的是同一个意思,但看起来却是再一次从正反两个方面有力地说明"聪明的朋友知道何时说真话,何时说假话"。

【写作语言分析】

关于主题句的主语问题

文章需要一个摆明作者总观点的句子,这个句子一般在第一段会出现。

在接下来的段落中,除了结尾段,topic sentence是我们每一段都必须有的纲领性句子。其出现的理想位置是段落之首,并且它一般都由两个部分组成:topic＋controlling meaning

用一个中文等号表示,就是:

$$主题句=主题(topic)+句子(controlling idea)$$
$$=主语+主语后面的部分$$
$$=说的是什么(describe)+怎么说的(prescribe)$$

因此,把一个主题句中的主语设置好,对于写出一个高级的主题句很重要。文章的第二、三自然段的主题句分别如下:

1) <u>The thing that most people are guilty of</u> is asking a question and expecting a specific response.

2) <u>Perhaps another thing that gives this away</u> is the asking of a question that cannot be answered correctly.

什么东西可以做主语呢? 这里使用的是两个稍微复杂的主语,大家可以学习一下。

1) 句使用的是定语从句

2) 句使用的依然是定语从句

可见,在主语中可以大胆地使用定语从句丰富句子意思。

范文五　教育的目的是什么

Think carefully about the issue presented in the following excerpt and the assignment below:

1. Education can't take the place of brains. To repeat what others have said requires education, to challenge it requires brains.
   Mary Pettibone Poole, *Collected Words*.

2. It is the mark of an educated mind to be able to entertain a thought without accepting it.

Assignment: Is the purpose of education to learn facts, to learn to have an open mind, or both? Plan and write an essay in which you develop your point of view on this issue. Support your position with reasoning and examples taken from your reading, studies, experience, or observation

6分范文：

In my many years of school, I've learned that teachers ideas about education. Some think that they need to cram your head with facts. Other poke and prod until students get their brains in gear and begin to think. From this second kind of teacher, I have learned the real meaning of education. It is learning to be able to form your own intelligent view of the world, based on both knowledge and a clear, open mind.

I used to be nervous and afraid of school. I studied all the time, trying to get as many facts as possible into my head. During class, I would break into a sweat in the rare moments that I didn't know an answer, just in case the teacher called on me for that question. Tests would upset my stomach.

But through all this work, I didn't really learn much. I don't remember all those names and dates and capital cities I memorized. I also couldn't tell you what my favorite books or poems or heroes were from that time. My learning had no real meaning for me. I didn't really stop and think about any of it, or interpret the information in my own personal way. I just tried to remember pages and pages of isolated facts.

Thanks to one great teacher, I no longer believe that this constitutes real learning. And I have an idea what does. It all came clear many years ago in Mr. Blumgarden's history class.

We were talking about the Civil War and the abolition of slavery. I was well prepared, of course. I knew all about the Battle of Antietam and the Battle of Bentonville, I could find the battlefields on a map and tell you how many people had died. I raised my hand to give an answer and Mr. Blumgarden called on me. After I had answered, he asked me another question. But this was an unusual question. He asked me what I thought soldiers on both sides thought about what they were fighting for. After that other people chimed in. And the class began to discuss the beliefs of both sides, the reason they went to war, and what might have happened if the other side had won. And I kept raising my hand, not to show how much I knew but, for once, because I was really interested.

I changed a lot in the course of that year. It started in history class as I realized that history is more than a string of names and dates. It's a story about people and the choices they make, and it's a story that can help us learn to be smart about our lives in the present. I started to relax a bit in all my classes and as I did, the others became more fun as well. We read Charles Dickens' "Oliver Twist" that year and I truly enjoyed it — it was funny and some of the characters reminded me of people I knew. I was learning how to learn, how to involve myself in the subjects and come to my own conclusions.

It was that year that my mind opened and I began to truly become educated. Rather than trying to fill my head with disconnected facts and other people's ideas, I now collect knowledge that I can use to form — or change — my opinions. And I plan to continue this my whole life, facing new situations with an educated, open mind.

【作者观点分析】

SAT 的提示,倘若有两句话,这两句话一般是互相支持的。本文也不例外。

第一句可翻译为:"教育无法替代大脑的思考。重复他人,我们需要教育;挑战他人,我们需要大脑。"

第二句可翻译为："受过教育的人的标志是他可以理解一种想法而不必要去接受它。"

从这两句看来，教育与独立思考似乎是两个对立面，无法融合。我们考生应该使用一种什么样的观点呢？

知识的特征有两个，第一个特点是它的继承性，即我们不管是与他人交谈，还是看书，或是从老师那里学习，首先要从他人那里得到初始的知识；第二个特点，就是它的创造性，失去了创造性的知识，是死知识，而失去了创造性的人，不是死人，是死脑筋。

因此，我们不能简单地在教育与独立思考间二选一，而应该是两者兼选，偏向独立思考为佳。

【文章内容分析】

文章第一段把 knowledge 与 a clear, open mind 相提并论，都放在形成一个正确的世界观（form your own intelligent view of the world）的重要地位。

文章从第二段到倒数第二段，使用的是一种非常轻松（当然不是口语化）的口吻，介绍了自己起初如何不懂得学习，而后来历史课上老师的提问，以及其他同学对于非记忆知识的投入，感染了他，让他认识到学习原来还这么有趣，认识到在背诵、死记事实背后还有更高的层次，让他经历了"背诵到理解"、"惧怕到爱好"的过程。这个过程并非平铺直叙，而是制造一个小小的悬念，抓住了读者的注意力。叙述的文笔是如此流畅，几乎让人一口气就读到文章最后。

文章的最后一句话"And I plan to continue this my whole life, facing new situations with an educated, open mind"也分别用"educated"和"open mind"暗暗呼应了第一段所提到的这两个事物上。倘若没有这句话，就无法体现出作者对内容收放自如的功力。

纵观全文，作者所讲述的内容其实非常常见，但是他的描述如此生动，可以让人忽略掉文章逻辑思维上并无深刻之处。但是，我们要知道，SAT 满分中，除去 critical thinking 这一要求，还有一个要求，就是 well organized and clearly focused, demonstrating clear coherence and smooth progressions of ideas。很显然，本文能够拿到满分明显胜在行文流畅，哪怕通篇都是说自己成长经历中的事情。

对于我们考生，这暗示着什么呢？有两个非常容易被人忽略的事实：

1. 如果你无法"深刻"，那么你可以"流畅"。

2. 你可以拿自己说事儿。在我们中国考生的思维中，最喜欢往大道理走，很忌讳说自己如何如何。可是在本书这几篇范文中，我们看到自己或自己身边普通人的例子并不鲜见。(范文二,"我妹妹"有天分不珍惜等于没天分;范文六,我去帮助老人反而被改变人生观;范文七,我排演节目的两种思路带来的不同效果。范文五、六、七,通篇只有一个例子,只有一个主角"我",但把主角的思想或内心变化过程描画得淋漓尽致,对比鲜明。)

美国文化与中国文化一个显著的区别,是对于 individualism 的不同理解。在美国文化中,对于"我"是值得研究的,有进步也是值得欢呼的。而我们中国学生,受到应试作文的思路影响,往往喜欢说某某说过什么,说中国的吧,老外考官很可能不知道;说西方的吧,自己能记得的不多,好容易记住的又怕张冠李戴。

既然"我"这么重要,为什么要舍近求远,舍易求难呢?

但写"我"时,千万要记得的是:第一,要扣紧题目的灵魂,不要成为日记体,流于肤浅。第二,一定要把我的"变化"写出来。

【写作语言分析】

用一种简单的语言也能得满分吗? 答案是肯定的。本文就是一例,通篇使用的词汇都比较简单,但并不呆板,流畅犹如小溪,活泼泼的,也惹人喜爱。

在这样的文章中,也有一些小小"潜规则",可供大家借鉴:

第一段结构不能太简单!"内容决定形式",第一段的功能是点出中心思想,这样的功能决定它不能太小儿科了,相对于中间的段落,它要庄重点,句式要长点,复杂点。本文第一段就使用了"I have learned the real meaning of education. It is learning to be able to form your own intelligent view of the world, based on both knowledge and a clear, open mind"这样一个长句子,对中心思想进行阐述。

在中间段落,句式可以随意啦!

以其中一段为例:

We were talking about the Civil War and the abolition of slavery. I was well prepared, of course. I knew all about the Battle of Antietam and the Battle of Bentonville, I could find the battlefields on a map and tell you how many people had died. I raised my hand to give an answer and Mr. Blumgarden called on me.

"We were . . ." "I was. ." "I knew . . ." "I cound find . . ." "I raised . . .",这样一连串以我开头的句子,非常的"自我中心",应该是要避免的,但在这种记述自己转变教育观念的文章中,这样的句子也无伤大雅。

最后一段,语言又要回归庄重。

It was that year that my mind opened and I began to truly become educated. Rather than trying to fill my head with disconnected facts and other people's ideas, I now collect knowledge that I can use to form — or change — my opinions. And I plan to continue this my whole life, facing new situations with an educated, open mind.

本文使用了强调句型"it was that","rather than",以及分词结构"facing new situations with an educated, open mind"等来显示庄重。

范文六　生命中最难忘的时刻是什么

Think carefully about the issue presented in the following excerpt and the assignment below:

1. The most important days of our lives are those in which we learn something new about ourselves. — *Jesse Pharios*

2. It's exhilarating to be alive in a time of awakening consciousness; it can also be confusing. — *Adrienne Rich*

Assignment: Is it true that the most memorable days of our lives are those in which we underwent some personal transformation or awakening? Plan and write an essay in which you develop your point of view on this issue. Support your position with reasoning and examples taken from your reading, studies, experience, or observation.

6 分范文:

People often complain that our generation is politically apathetic. Just 25 years ago, it was common for students to join in strikes and antiwar protests, but nowadays, the stereotype goes, young people are more likely to be found watching MTV or shopping at the mall. I certainly was no different. Appallingly ignorant of current events, I never read a paper or watched the news, but I knew all about the personal lives of popular TV and movie stars. Then something happened to change my outlook forever.

In my social studies class, we had an assignment to interview an older person about the changes he or she had witnessed in his or her lifetime. I decided to interview my neighbor, Mrs. Fletcher. Since she had never spoken to me much before, I figured she would have little to say and I could complete the assignment quickly. Instead she started telling me all about life in our town before the civil rights movement. I was astonished to learn that in the 1950s, black went to separate schools, rode at the backs of buses, and were prevented from living in white neighborhoods. As Mrs. Fletcher talked about how she and other African

Americans helped break the color barrier by insisting on being served at white-only lunch counters, I became filled with shame at my own ignorance. How could I have been so unaware?

From that moment onward, politics and history became my passions. In school we had been taught that there was no society freer than the United States, but that was only part of the story. By reading about the political struggles of minorities, women, blue-collar workers, and others, I learned that freedom is not something you're given, it's something you have to fight for. And once you win it, you have to make sure no one tries to take it away again. I learned so much from Mrs. Fletcher that day, and our conversation transformed me forever. I developed an awareness of the world around me, became less self-absorbed, and took a very important lesson from the past: progress begins with people who choose to stand up for what is right. It was like I'd had a rebirth after talking with Mrs. Fletcher, and that is why I agree with the idea that the most memorable days of our lives are those in which we learn something new about ourselves and experience an awakening.

【作者观点分析】

Adrienne Cecile Rich 是美国著名的女权主义者、诗人和散文家,出生于 1929 年,被称为 20 世纪后期最有影响力的诗人。

她的生平也可以说是女性觉醒、对自身角色重新认识的一个缩影。她 24 岁与 Alfred Haskell Conrad 结婚,育有三子,使得她无法专注于自己的写作,这种状态也让她觉得不满足(These conflicting roles and ambitions left her unfulfilled)。1966 年移居到纽约后,她日渐投入到社会的变化中去(Rich moved with her family, which then included three sons, to New York City and became increasingly involved in the sociopolitical activism of the day)。她首先投入学生运动及反战运动,60 到 70 年代投入女性运动。1964 年,她加入了 New Left 组织,使得她在政治与个人方面变得成熟(spurred a period of both political and personal growth),最终成为反战积极分子和女权运动中比较激进的女权主义者。不得不提及的是,她丈夫在与她分居后不久,于 1970 年自杀。早在 1963 年,她就在自己的作品中,对自己的女性身份进行反思(examine her female identity),而她也于 1976 年,通过自己的引起争议的作品 *Of Woman Born: Motherhood as Experience and Institution* 向世人公开了她的同性恋倾向。

为什么要介绍这些东西呢?因为我们这篇满分作文的作者,看似轻松地与一位老人拉家常,其实暗中传达这样一个讯息——"我深刻理解这段名言,我甚至了解这段名言背后的故事,我对美国历史和文学有一定的知识"。

这也是为什么,同样是写个人的成长,有的人就可以拿满分,有的人却不行。因为,我们作为考生要讲的故事,必须要与名言有关才有可能拿高分。换句话说,要想方设法在自己讲的故事中,扯上与美国历史、文化和文学有关的一些背景知识,让考官看到你的知识底蕴。

我们已经在前面了解到,SAT考试不是简单的语言考试,而是美国大学优中选优的考试。因此,不同于着重点在语言方面的托福和雅思,它的高分作文一定符合一个标准,就是critical thinking(批判性的思维),并要严谨;倘若能体现出对美国历史人文知识的了解,那就是锦上添花了。

美国历史虽然不是很长很复杂,但美国20世纪60年代,作为一个特殊的动荡的年代,各种思想浪潮此起彼伏。大家可能都熟悉的马丁·路德·金博士的"I have a dream"。他领导了黑人要求平等权利的民权运动并为此献身。除了这个运动,同时代的还有年轻人的反越战运动,大学生的要求自治运动,妇女的要求平等运动等等……在这些运动的影响下,当时的美国社会呈现出完全不同的风貌。因此,我们要了解美国,就不能不了解这段美国年轻人以天下为己任、参与缔造历史的特殊时期。

【文章内容分析】

本文最大的特点就是landmark用得非常的清晰。也就是说,在每一段的开头都有明确的topic sentence进行预告——我这段将会讲什么内容。在每段结束时,能尽量再次用不同的语言进行归纳总结。

第一段,指出现在的小孩不像以往那样对政治有积极的兴趣,而是回避甚至厌恶政治(People often complain that our generation is politically apathetic),"我"也一样,但是"我"被一件小事彻底改变了(something happened to change my outlook forever)。行文至此,悬念产生——到底是什么事情呢?

第二段,讲"我"上社会课,要去询问老人所经历过的改变(we had an assignment to interview an older person about the changes he or she had witnessed)。这个事情,就把个人与社会挂钩,把现在与过去挂钩,高明!然后就是一幅对比鲜明的画面——有个懵懂的少年与一位风烛残年的老人在一起,听老人讲述曾经的热血过往。

第三段,讲这个事件对我的改变(From that moment onward, politics and history became my passions)。

注意!这个时候你必须用上"美国人爱看的句子"。

也许你会有疑问,什么句子是"美国人爱看的句子"呢?很简单,好莱坞大片中经常会出现的一些句子,就是美国背景的人最爱看到的句子,包括看你卷子的美国考官。

有一个句子是：这只是故事的一半（but that was only part of the story）。为什么喜欢这句子？因为美国文化最讨厌的是人云亦云，最欢迎的是 critical thinking。因此，如果你说这只是故事的一半，那么他就很喜欢你的全面思维。

还有一个句子是：自由不是天上掉下来的，要去争取，甚至战斗（Freedom is not something you're given, it's something you have to fight for）。为什么喜欢这句子？因为美国本来不是一个国家，是从英国手里经过了独立战争打下来的；美国的国家特点之一也不是中央集权，而是联邦制，州政府与联邦政府之间的权利分配也是斗争的结果；美国的三权分立本质上也是政府各个部门权利互相制约而达到平衡，目的是防止独裁……因此，为自己的权利而战，为自己的自由而战，这一向是好莱坞的主题，也是美国文化的核心价值。

本段出现了两个与题目相关又暗合考官心思的好句子，当然可以得高分。

本段结束时，也就是全文结束时，用了"that is why I agree with the idea that ＋重复主题思想"这样的模式进行全文总结，也再次点题，非常有力。

【写作语言分析】

作为参加美国高考的学生，我们不可能期待考生们有多么深刻的思想；如果是那样的话，考生也不需要大学的培养，直接可以走上社会了。那么，考生如何吸引住考官的注意力呢？对于一个观点，可以使用不同的词汇进行解释、强化。丰富的语言与词汇，可使简单的思想有趣，甚至显得多姿多彩。SAT 满分作文有一个要求：exhibits skillful use of language, using a varied, accurate, and apt vocabulary（通过运用多变、准确、得体的词汇，展示较高的语言技巧）。

比如说，本文作者在描述 60 年代的年轻人与现在的年轻人的对比中，就使用了大量的相关词汇进行形象的描述，有抽象，有具体，两者对比一下就活起来了。

60 年代的年轻人	现在的年轻人
join in strikes	politically apathetic（抽象）
(join in) antiwar protects	watching MTV or shopping at the mall
	appallingly ignorant of current events（抽象）
	never read a paper or watched the news
	know all about the personal lives of popular TV and movie stars

又比如，在第三段最后几句话，描写自己变化时，就连续使用了以下黑体划线部分的词语，进行同一观点的连续强化，让考官觉得，"这孩子真不容易，变这么上进了，还是给高分吧。"

... **transformed** me forever. I **developed an awareness of** the world around me, **became less self-absorbed**, and took a very important lesson from the past: progress begins with people who choose to stand up for what is right. It was like I'd had a **rebirth** ...

范文七 过去的经历对未来的作用

Think carefully about the issue presented in the following excerpt and the assignment below.

> Many persons believe that to move up the ladder of success and achievement, they must forget the past, repress it, and relinquish it. But others have just the opposite view. They see old memories as a chance to reckon with the past and integrate past and present.
>
> — Adapted from Sara Lawrence-Lightfoot, *I've Known Rivers: Lives of Loss and Liberation*

Assignment: Do memories hinder or help people in their effort to learn from the past and succeed in the present? Plan and write an essay in which you develop your point of view on this issue. Support your position with reasoning and examples taken from your reading, studies, experience, or observations.

6 分作文：

Without our past, our future would be a tortuous path leading to nowhere. In order to move up the ladder of success and achievement we must come to terms with our past and integrate it into our future. Even if in the past we made mistakes, this will only make wiser people out of us and guide us to where we are supposed to be.

This past year, I was auditioning for the fall play, "Cat on a Hot Tin Roof." To my detriment I thought it would be a good idea to watch the movie in order to prepare. For two hours I studied Elizabeth Taylor's mannerisms, attitude, and diction, hoping I could mimic her performance. I auditioned for the part of "Maggie" feeling perfectly confident in my portrayal of Elizabeth Taylor, however, I was unaware that my director saw exactly what I had been thinking. Unfortunately, I didn't get the part, and my director told me that he needed to see "Maggie" from my perspective, not Elizabeth Taylor's.

I learned from this experience, and promised myself I would not try to imitate another actress, in order to create my character. Persevering, I was anxious to audition for the winter play just two months later. The play was Neil Simon's "Rumors," and would get the opportunity to play "Chris," a sarcastic yet witty role, which would be my final performance in high school. In order to develop my character, I planned out her life just as I thought it should be, gave her the voice I thought was right, and the rest of her character unfolded beautifully from there. My director told me after the first show that "Rumors" was the best work he'd ever seen from me, and that he was amazed at how I'd developed such a believable character. Thinking back to my first audition I was grateful for that chance I had to learn and to grow, because without that mistake I might have tried to base "Chris" off of someone I'd known or something I'd seen instead of becoming my own character. I utilized the memory of the Elizabeth Taylor debacle to improve my approach to acting and gave the best performance of my life so far.

【作者观点分析】

怎样提出中心思想呢？提出中心思想可以开门见山，也可以先抑后扬。"文似看山不喜平"，我们可以考虑使用抑扬结合的手法提出观点。

比如说，第四篇范文"人们都希望听到真心回答吗"，使用的结构是：第一句话反对观点"Most people ... will say that ... "＋"Is this really true?"＋接下来提出自己的观点。

同样，本文第一句话是作者反对观点（Without ＋作者反对的观点），第二句话是自己的观点，也小小地"不平"了一下。

作者的观点"In order to move up the ladder of success and achievement we must come to terms with our past and integrate it into our future"，对于过去的态度是"come to terms"并且"integrate into future"。

作者是怎样证明这个观点的呢？他通过自身作为演员的一次失败和一次成功的经历，证明从过去失败经历中吸取经验教训对于成功的重要性。

两次经历中间，分水岭一样的"I learned from this experience, and promised myself I would not try to imitate another actress, in order to create my character. "使得文章脉络清楚，让人喜欢。（句子内部可以多拐几个弯，而整个文章的观点要清楚，要么对比鲜明，要么干脆一边倒。如果你在文章各大段落使用太多的 yet, however, but，反而会把考官弄糊涂了，不知道你到底转了几次弯，而直接把你的作文判死刑。）

【文章内容分析】

文章阐述了自己的成长过程,行文流畅,发展合理,紧扣核心内容,令人信服地证明了"从过去的失败中吸取教训有助于将来的成功"这样一个道理。

在范文五"教育的目的是什么?"中我们提到过,内容可以是自己的,欢迎讲自己生动有趣的成长故事。

【写作语言分析】

本文第一段使用了箴言一样理性的语言,平实,富于哲理而不失优美。如何做到思维活泼且严谨? 我们可以通过灵活句子结构来实现。

要记住两句话。其一:"句首,兵家必争之地。"

每个分句都承载着已知信息与新信息。对于新信息的位置,英语与汉语有明显不同——在英语中,新信息多半在结尾,但受句法框架限制,不在结尾的也不少;而汉语中新信息总在结尾,否则意思不明朗。

这说明,我们可以使得我们的写作更地道——在句首使用分词、动名词、不定式,使句首丰富起来!

其二:"句尾,平静补充之地。"

在句尾多使用分词进行补充说明,使内容摇曳多姿!

<u>Without our past</u>, our future would be a tortuous path <u>leading to nowhere</u>. <u>In order to</u> move up the ladder of success and achievement we must come to terms with our past and integrate it into our future. <u>Even if</u> in the past we made mistakes, this will only make wiser people out of us and guide us to where we are supposed to be.

Without our past, 强调句式,放在句首表强调;

In order to move up the ladder of success and achievement, 不定式,放在句首表目的;

Even if in the past we made mistakes, 让步状语从句,放在句首表示让步;

leading to nowhere, 分词短语放在句尾表补充说明。

再看看另外一段:

<u>To my detriment</u> I thought it would be a good idea to watch the movie in order to prepare. <u>For two hours</u> I studied Elizabeth Taylor's mannerisms, attitude, and diction, <u>hoping I could mimic her performance.</u> I auditioned for the part of "Maggie" <u>feeling perfectly confident in my portrayal of Elizabeth Taylor</u>, however, I was unaware that my director . . .

To my detriment 是强调句式,放在句首表强调;

For two hours 是强调句式, 放在句首表强调;

hoping I could mimic her performance, 分词形式的动宾结构, 放在句尾表补充说明;

feeling perfectly confident in my portrayal of Elizabeth Taylor, 分词放在句尾表补充说明。

注意! 要避免出现悬垂结构。也就是分词、动名词、不定式三类非谓语动词做状语时, 其逻辑主语与主句逻辑主语不一致。

比如:

To prepare for the final examination, the room was crowded.　　　[×]

To prepare for the final examination, students crowded the classroom.　[√]

Hearing a number of interesting stories, our visit was thoroughly enjoyable.

　　　　　　　　　　　　　　　　　　　　　　　　　　　　　　[×]

Hearing a number of interesting stories, we thoroughly enjoyed our visit.　[√]

On entering the room, candies were being served.　　　　　　　　[×]

On entering the room, I found that candies were being served.　　　[√]

范文八 评判英雄的标准

Think carefully about the issue presented in the following excerpt and the assignment below:

> Traditionally the term "heroism" has been applied to those who have braved physical danger to defend a cause or to protect others. But one of the most feared dangers people face is that of disapproval by their family, peers, or community. Sometimes acting courageously requires someone to speak out at the risk of such rejection. We should consider those who do so true heroes.

Assignment: Should heroes be defined as people who say what they think when we ourselves lack the courage to say it? Plan and write an essay in which you develop your point of view on this issue. Support your position with reasoning and examples taken from your reading, studies, experience, or observation.

6分作文:

There are many types of heroes in real life or in literature, but the most courageous type of all is the one who is willing to stand up and say what they believe in even when everyone else lacks the courage to do so. Many people are content to go through life following the crowd. They will themselves believe in ideas that society says is right, even when they know in their heart it is wrong. A hero is one who is willing to give up his position in society in order to tell people what he believes is right.

The abolitionists, such as Harriet Beecher Stowe and William Iloyd Garrison, were heroes in their own time. Before the Civil War, people in all sections of the country thought that African Americans were animals and treated them as such. During the reform period of the Jacksonian era William Iloyd Garrison began to publish his abolitionist newspaper The Liberator. In this newspaper he demanded that the African American slaves be set free immediately, without any compensation to their owners. Because his view on slavery was against the common belief of the population he was not received well. Throughout his life he was given multiple death threats and one of his abolitionist friends was killed. Harriet Beecher Stowe was an abolitionist after Garrison's time, but she was received in much of the same way. After the Fugitive Slave Act of 1850 was released, she wrote the book *Uncle* Tom's *Cabin*. It was a story of a slave living in the South and the cruelty of his owner. The inhumanness of the owner caused many southerners to ban the book in anger, but at the same time it brought the terrible act of slavery to the light. Many northerners used this book as a weapon against the South's peculiar institution.

Rudyard Kipling once wrote in his poem, which said that you will be a man if you can stand up and say what you believe in when all men around you doubt you. Heroes must have the courage to risk everything they love to stand up for theirselves in the face of opposition. Both William Iloyd Garrison and Harriet Beecher Stowe stood up against a society which had accepted slavery as a right. They believed that what their heart told them was right and risked everything to tell the public what they believed in. These two people have hopefully shown others to believe in themselves and what they view in their hearts.

【作者观点分析】

提示中问的是"Should heroes be defined as people who say what they think when we ourselves lack the courage to say it?"从我们中国考生的角度看这个问题有点拗口,不妨用另外一个问题来代替它,看看它是个 argument 还是 report。

"What is the definition for a hero?"

A hero can be defined as a person who say what he/she thinks when others lack the courage to say it.

Bingo!

看出来了,本文是一篇 report 式的文章,需要阐明"什么是真正的英雄",而且答案已经给出来了,那就是"决不人云亦云"。

【文章内容分析】

相对而言,report 不需要脑筋转来转去,没有两个观点你死我活的争斗,只需要"下定义＋举例子＋收尾段"就行了。

开篇第一段可以采用"正＋反＋正"的套路提出作者对于"英雄"的定义;

There are many types of XXX...

Some...(the type that the author does not approve)

(Yet) a hero is one who ... (give definition for XXX)

中间的段落最常见的是举例说明;对于这种文章,思辨性方面的要求降低了,但信息量要求上升了。也就是说,举的例子一定要非常有代表性,要么是历史上有名的人或事件,要么是身边比较耳熟能详的人物。

本文作者举的例子是在南北战争时期,在解放黑奴运动中做出了杰出贡献的两位先驱——一位是在 1931 年创办激进废奴主义杂志《解放者》,并提出"立刻无条件释放黑奴"的加里逊,一位是 1852 年发表《汤姆叔叔的小屋》,被林肯称赞为"发动我们伟大内战的小女人"的斯托夫人。

结尾段落再次提到中间的例子,说明例子符合第一段的定义。

【写作语言分析】

使用一种"老到"的语言在 SAT 作文中更容易出彩,往往受到评卷老师的青睐。那么,如何样才能老到呢?

我们在前面的范文分析中已经谈到过,灵活变化句子结构,注意过渡词语及标志性过渡句子的使用等,能让文章显得变化丰富,摇曳生姿。如:

Histories make men wise; poets witty; the mathematics subtile; natural philosophy deep; moral grave; logic and rhetoric able to contend. Abeunt studia in morse. ("读史使人明智,读诗使人灵秀,数学使人周密,科学使人深刻,伦理学使人庄重,逻辑修辞之学使人善辩;凡有所学,皆成性格。"——培根)

我们从文章的举例段,看看作者掌握了多么丰富的历史知识,并且灵活穿插,自成一体。划线部分是对历史事实的客观陈述,能体现作者广泛的阅读面与精准的记忆。

The abolitionists, such as Harriet Beecher Stowe and William Iloyd Garrison, were heroes in their own time. Before the Civil War, people in all sections of the country thought that African Americans were animals and treated them as such. During the reform period of the Jacksonian era William Iloyd Garrison began to publish his abolitionist newspaper *The Liberator*. In this newspaper he demanded that the African American slaves be set free immediately, without any compensation to their owners. Because his view on slavery was against the common belief of the population he was not received well. Throughout his life he was given multiple death threats and one of his abolitionist friends was killed.

Harriet Beecher Stowe was an abolitionist after Garrison's time, but she was received in much of the same way. After the Fugitive Slave Act of 1850 was released, she wrote the book *Uncle Tom's Cabin*. It was a story of a slave living in the South and the cruelty of his owner. The inhumanness of the owner caused <u>many southerners to ban the book</u> in anger, but at the same time it brought the terrible act of slavery to the light. Many northerners used this book as a weapon against the <u>South's peculiar institution.</u>

　　我们前面提到过，要多留意历史知识，尤其是美国历史的一些重要时期，如独立战争时期，南北战争时期，以及 20 世纪 60 年代等等。在这里，我们还要强调，在平时阅读有关美国历史文章的时候，应该把一些关键的历史事实掌握准确，这样就可以在引用这些事例的时候，轻松拈来。这些史实尤如珍珠，等待有心人去拾纳，在恰当的时候，穿针引线，成就完美之作。

　　"不积跬步，无以至千里，不积小流，无以成江河"。中国考生对于美国历史方面的阅读，一来有畏难情绪，二来比较缺乏系统学习的动力，一直比较薄弱。阅读是写作的基础，我们必须有针对性地阅读相关的美国历史，并把相关内容熟记在心！

范文九 是行动还是语言反映
人们的真实面目

> Think carefully about the issue presented in the following excerpt and the assignment below:
>
> > Governments, businesses, groups, or people reveal themselves by how they act, not by what they say. A company may claim to value its customers, or a politician may claim to be committed to a cause, but what do their actions say? People or groups may state what they wish were true or what they think others want to hear, but it is their actions that reveal their true values.
>
> **Assignment:** Do actions, not words, reveal a person or a group's true attitudes and intentions? Plan and write an essay in which you develop your point of view on this issue. Support your position with reasoning and examples taken from your reading, studies, experience, or observation.

6分作文：

Actions, not words, reveal a person's or a group's true attitude and intention. This can be witnessed on three different spectrums — companies, politicians, and students. It is what each do that truly state the person's or group's values.

Companies often use advertisement to create an amicable image. For example, tobacco companies agree to advertise the health concerns related to tobacco usage, but is that really what the company wants to offer? No, these companies do not care about health issues; instead, they wish to sell as many tobacco products as possible. For that reason, the board meetings of those companies often focus on the clever ways to circumvent the legal and health restrictions posed on their products. What they say is not what they wish to do.

Moreover, politicians rely solely on a positive image. By speaking eloquently about their hopeful and flowery proposals, politicians have developed a superb skill of publicity. But once again, do politicians really speak of their intention? Most can argue that they try to remain on their goals set on public hearings, but we all can agree that the politicians can not maintain their intended spoken goals for too long. Soon, the politicians will revert back to what they all want — power and continuous popularity. For example, George. W. Bush have been saying he will end the war in the Middle East since 2003. Now, in 2008, the war is continuing raging fervently. His words intended to end, but his actions further exacerbated the problems. Although he has debated that his behaviour were intend to make USA a better place, his actions proved to be futile in solving the problem. His actions reflected his true intentions.

Students, on the other hand, also do not say what they really intend to do. Their actions are the only reliable way through which one can understand their true attitudes. For example, my friend Tom has such a case. In school, he agrees to the teachers every recommendation; whether it is studying for upcoming test or doing an extra research project, he will willingly nod to the requests. However, after school, his actions differ. He will always phone others to go partying with him. He spends his weekends at arcades and restaurants eating lavish dinners. One thing he doesn't do is studying. That was the thing he initially set out to do.

In conclusion, companies, politicians and students have one thing in common: their actions reveal their true nature and intentions. Whatever they say, regardless how convincing, will be overpowered by their actions, the true indication of their attitudes.

【作者观点分析】

这篇文章是比较典型的中式思维的文章，一板一眼的思维，中规中矩的文风，虽然少点活泼，但也可以接受。毕竟大家都是中式家庭长大，总觉得前面所说的那些"讲述老百姓自己的故事"有点玄，不太可能在看了我们这本书后就都开始"拿自己说事"。那么，好吧，就从大道理开讲。SAT 考官不太欢迎古板的文章，所以请你一定要说得严谨，展示你缜密的思维。

毫无悬念，作者的观点，也就是文章的中心思想即开头第一句话"Actions, not words, reveal a person's or a group's true attitude and intention"，然后告诉读者，本文将从公司、政客、学生三个方面阐述。

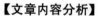

【文章内容分析】

本文为什么能打高分呢？

本文胜在古板的帽子下面，有表情丰富的脸蛋。也就是说，每个段落举的例子都很贴切、生动！

第一段，讲公司的时候，例子是烟草公司。(... tobacco companies agree to advertise the health concerns related to tobacco usage, but ... (they) do not care about health issues; instead, they wish to sell as much tobacco products as possible.)

第二段，讲政客的时候，以美国前总统小布什在伊拉克战争问题上的出尔反尔为例。(For example, George. W. Bush have been saying he will end the war in the Middle East since 2003. Now, in 2008, the war is continuing raging fervently. His words intended to end, but his actions further exacerbated the problems.)

第三段，讲学生，以作者身边贪玩的学生 Tom 为例。(In school, he agrees to the teachers every recommendation; ... However, after school, his actions differ.)

总结段，文章把三个方面收入囊中，概括了三类人的一个共性：行动反映他们的真实本性与想法(their actions reveal their true nature and intentions)。最后一句话(Whatever they say, regardless how convincing, will be overpowered by their actions, the true indication of their attitudes.)使用了一个漂亮的插入语 regardless（应该是 regardless of how convincing），还使用了一个很贴切的动词 A is overpowered by B,内容与中心思想毫无二致。虽然重复，但也算是再一次强调作者的观点吧。

【写作语言分析】

汉语的语言现象，我们常说，以"主题"为核心，"竹节式"发展。我们可能不容易找到主题句，但"形散神不散"。

英文中有一个常见但很有趣的现象，就是"形聚神聚"。一个句子以"主语"为核心，进行"葡萄式"发展。类似的，一个意群，一个段落，以核心句为中心，进行"1＋N"发展。我们可以非常容易地在一个段落中找到中心句及若干个支撑句子。注意，N 个句子内部可能又有 n 个小句子对它们进行支撑，请看下列结构：

　　　　1＋ 分论点 1＋支撑分论点 1 的几个句子；

　　　　　　分论点 2＋支撑分论点 1 的几个句子；

　　　　　　……

　　　　　　分论点 N＋支撑分论点 N 的几个句子；

我们可以用七个字来简单概括上面复杂的方程式——**"写一句,三句支撑"**。

在这里,我们不再讨论主题句的重要性,而是让大家注意,在SAT高分作文中,有这样一种写法,即在一个段落中,说一个意思,然后用两三句支撑。

为了方便大家理解,我们在下面使用了一个结构图对文章的举例段进行说明。箭头后面的方框,就是对前面方框内容的支撑。

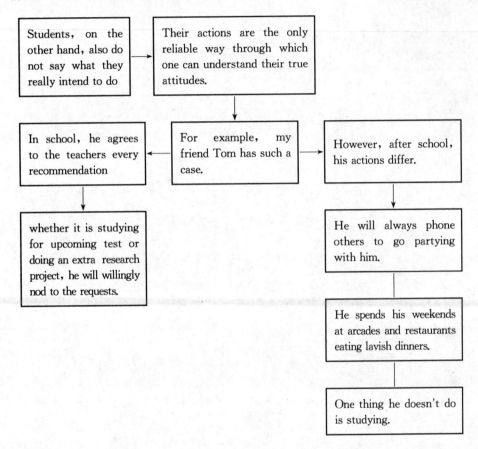

附记:

这是 2008 年 10 月的 SAT 考题,笔者的一名学生凭这篇作文一举拿下满分 12 分。总的来说,这篇满分文章还存在着这样那样的小问题,特别是一些小的文法错误,但由于作者思维缜密,举例恰当,同时用词比较典雅,反映了他具有一定的英文表达能力,所以最后拿到了满分。

在用词方面,第二段里使用了 amicable、circumvent、pose(作者笔误,应该是 imposed),第三段使用了 eloquently、raging fervently、exacerbated the problem、futile。这些词相对比较大了,属于 big words,但在句子中使用得恰到好处,所以并没有炫耀词汇量之嫌。这也证明了,用词不在于大小,关键是用在句子里是否恰当。西方的老师往往让学生写得越简单越好,笔者对这点也一直持有不同看法,翻翻 TIME 之类的杂志就不难明白,用大词很多时候也是文章的需要。

这篇充满着浓厚中式风格的文章非常值得同学们去学习,既然讲不好故事,就以理服人,把文章写得中规中矩,这也不失为一种写好文章的方法。

范文十 坚持还是放弃——当你没有进展时

Think carefully about the issue presented in the following excerpt and the assignment below:

> The history of human achievement is filled with stories of people who persevere, refusing to give up in the struggle to meet their goals. Artists and scientists, for instance, may struggle for years without any apparent progress or reward before they finally succeed. However, it is important to recognize that perseverance does not always yield beneficial result.
>
> Adapted from Robert H. Lauer and Jeanette C. Lauer, *Watersheds*

Assignment: Is striving to achieve a goal always the best course of action, or should people give up if they are not making progress? Plan and write an essay in which you develop your point of view on this issue. Support your position with reasoning and examples taken from your reading, studies, experience, or observations.

6 分作文：

We are born to this world to fight a war, a war that demands our time, ambition and enduring perseverance. This war has a name that shines upon our road of progressing-success. This war can be varied-from personal goals to national goals. Yet, no matter how big, how far, and how hard these goals are, we should always strive to achieve them under whatsoever situations. Only through this fearless and unremitting process, we are truly making our ways to success.

Some may argue a counterpoint that a judicious individual should know when to give up when he or she is not making any progress. Yet, in the course of human history, we can see too many brilliant examples in which individuals did not give up and eventually encountered success. The 16th U. S president, Abraham Lincoln, had encountered a series of hapless events before he was elected: his mother, sister and sons died successively; he encountered two bankruptcies; he failed to be elected as a senator; his father didn't support his dream to be erudite. Nevertheless, in the face of these difficulties, Lincoln never quit. His perseverance truly embeds the American spirit.

Perhaps we can also looked at a bigger scope-a national goal. Until Lincoln signed the Emancipation Proclamation, slavery was pervasive in U. S. Throughout the century, countless abolitionists strived to free the slaves and reach the humanity in the country. If they were to give up when no one supported them, would we still call them judicious individuals when all of us today can enjoy the equal opportunity regardless of our races?

Success is a seemingly insurmountable mountain and we are explorers who dream of seeing the beautiful landscape behind this mountain. Sometimes the conditions are difficult and some of us quit the journey, asserting that they make the right decision. Yet the truth is, those of us who strive through the journey finally see the heavenly and beautiful landscape, and those who give up lament with pity voices, asking themselves-why did I give up when I can continue?

【作者观点分析】

提示中给了两种观点：人类进步史上，很多人都是坚持不懈才赢得最后的胜利；但我们也要看到，坚持并不是都能带来好结果。

题目看起来是有两面，但只能写"坚持"这个方面。为什么呢？虽然说你的观点不重要，但坚持就是胜利是妇孺皆知的事实，你要选择反面来写，首先例子很难找，另外，多少也给阅卷者留下个不好的印象。所以，对这类老生常谈的题目，还是采取保守的态度比较有把握。

【文章内容分析】

一般而言，应试文章的开头和结尾两段有比较固定的内容。开头要提出现象、点出作者的观点，结尾要再次点题、重申作者观点。这样，如何在中间的两到三个自然段中，把自己的思路清晰而有特色地阐述出来，就非常考验考生组织观点的能力及扩展段落的能力了。也就是说，我们要分两步走，先"收"，后"放"。

首先，我们讲"收"。

比如说，"坚持还是放弃"这个题目非常大，难免落于空洞。因此，我们必须把题目缩小到可以把握的点上(narrow the topic mercilessly)。

下图形象地展示作者的思路，如何一步步把话题变得非常方便讨论。作者采用的是"证实"的思路，也就是提出一个证据来证明自己的观点。林肯的事例虽然大家都知道，但文章作者强悍的文风使得这个普通的证据也具有凌厉感，不容反驳。

坚持还是放弃

↓

坚持的几点好效果

↓

坚持在个人生活和社会发展中的作用

↓

为什么有的人可以当总统，因为他坚持

↓

林肯的坚持怎样让他当上了总统，改变美国命运

其次，我们讲"放"。

所谓"放"，绝对不是无的放矢的"放"，而是围绕文章的 main idea，从另外的角度继续阐述。

比如说本文，就以林肯的事例讲了个人和国家两个层次，是一种非常有层次感的"放"。第二段中心句就是从个人层次提出观点"we can see too many brilliant examples in which <u>individuals</u> did not give up and eventually <u>encountered</u> success"。第三段中心句从国家层次提出观点"Perhaps we can also looked at a bigger scope-a national goal"。

下面是作者如何展开"林肯"范例的总结。

Personal level	National level
hapless events	the Emancipation Proclamation
his mother, sister and sons died successively	slavery was pervasive
He encountered two bankruptcies	abolitionists
he failed to be elected as a senator	strived to free the slaves
his father didn't support his dream to be erudite	enjoy the equal opportunity regardless of our races

【写作语言分析】

在某些场合，我们可以使用一种有"气场"的语言，达到震慑人的目的，在 5 秒钟内把考官"电晕"，让他在一种迷糊的状态下打出高分。

如何达到这种目的呢？

1. 用有气势的词汇（比如和太阳有关的 shine，与命运有关的 be born to，与战争有关的 fight a war，与强权有关的 demand 等等）。

2. 使用加强语气的副词。

3. 连续使用近义词、排比。

以文章第一段为例：

We <u>are born to this world</u>（有气势的词汇）to <u>fight a war</u>（有气势的词汇），a war that <u>demands</u>（有气势的词汇）our <u>time，ambition and enduring perseverance</u>（排比）. This war has a name that <u>shines upon</u>（有气势的词汇）our road of progressing-success. ... Yet，no matter <u>how big，how far，and how hard</u>（排比）these goals are，we should always strive to achieve them under <u>whatsoever</u>（加强语气的副词）situations. Only through this <u>fearless and unremitting</u>（连续使用近义词）process，we are <u>truly</u>（加强语气的副词）making our ways to success.

尽管还只是高中毕业生，本文作者从文章第一段开始就表现出了高于普通学生的鼓动力与号召力。从本文的第一段看出，文风颇类似于美国总统的演说稿，用一种如雷贯耳的穿透力，把作者要表达的意思完全表达出来。我们仿佛听到了肯尼迪总统说：

"Ask not what your country can do for you，but what you can do for your country. "

需要注意的是，风格应该全文统一，不可以一下子庄重，一下子又口语味十足。如在本文最后一段，大家可以看到，作者还是保持了那种酷酷的文风。

Success is a <u>seemingly insurmountable</u>[1] mountain and we are explorers who dream of seeing the beautiful landscape behind this mountain. Sometimes the conditions are difficult and some of us quit the journey，<u>asserting that they make the right decision</u>[2]. Yet the truth is，<u>those of us who strive through the journey finally see the heavenly and beautiful landscape，and those who give up lament with pity voices，asking themselves — why did I give up when I can continue?</u>[3]

本段有三个特点使得它成为典型的正式文体。

1. 定语不怕冗长。

对于 success，作者使用了"副词＋形容词"修饰的结构（seemingly insurmountable），显得很冗长，但这是正式文风的特点之一。同样后面出现了"heavenly and beautiful landscape"，也是类似的结构。

2. 多使用分词、不定式、独立结构进行灵活修饰。

asserting that they make the right decision 属于一种独立结构，表伴随状态，放在句子结尾，这也非常正式。

类似的，lament with pity voices，asking themselves-why did I give up when I can continue 也是使用分词结构对 those who give up 进行描述。

3. 句子长而不乱，结构清晰。

比如最后一个句子中 the truth is 后面的三行话，就是 truth 的整个内容，对比的内容中间使用 and 进行连接，层次分明（当然，while 比 and 更好）。

另外，这种有"气场"的文风，属于一种政治味比较浓的风格，此处与林肯的事例正好相符；倘若考生连基本的风格都扯不清楚，还是平实点好，否则邯郸学步，满篇大话，反而不好了。

附记：

这是 2009 年 1 月的 SAT 考试作文题，笔者的一名学生凭借其深厚的英文功底和扎实的背景知识，一举拿下满分。全文气势恢宏，句式庄重，用词典雅，让阅卷者心服口服，不得不给满分。同时，文章的举例也反映了作者深厚的历史功底。

第三章 12篇SAT作文
修改及点评

收集在这里的12篇文章,全部出自笔者的学生之手,凡作文附有分数的,系考生参加SAT考试的作品。所有作文,笔者一字未改(除部分明显笔误之外)。

这些学生的背景基本上都是从小在中文环境下长大,他们的作文多多少少都带有中文的痕迹。为了让读者有所收获,收集在这里的作文基本上都是问题比较多的,并且这些问题,对华人学生来说,具有一定的共性。

文章的修改侧重于文字表达及文法错误,我们在10篇优秀范文里就文章的内容分析较多,而本章不侧重内容分析。

希望同学们仔细研读分析部分,看看这些问题在自己的英文写作中是否存在,不断纠正自己的语法错误,不断提高自己的文字表达能力。这不仅仅对SAT作文有所帮助,对正式进入美国大学学习也是大有裨益的。

第一篇 我们对公众人物是否期待太多

Think carefully about the issue presented in the following excerpt and the assignment below.

The price of greatness is responsibility.

— Winston Churchill

Assignment: Do we expect too much from our public figures? Plan and write an essay in which you develop your point of view on this issue. Support your position with reasoning and examples taken from your reading, studies, experience, or observations.

【学生原作】

Public figures always seem to raise <u>controversial issues①</u> <u>when they appear on the news②</u>. People tend to magnify every detail about their speeches, clothing, and <u>actions③</u>. <u>As the standard of satisfaction grows at an amazing rate, perfection seems to be easily attainable, and therefore generally expected.④</u> Sports stars, singers, and politicians often <u>disguise themselves from who they really are⑤</u> <u>in order to gain acceptance⑥</u>. As a result, too little tolerance is given to our public figures. The following examples of Liu Xiang and The Beetles demonstrate how people place way too heavy expectations on those who are <u>in public gazes⑦</u>.

① controversial issues 可以直接使用 controversies 代替。

② when they appear on the news：明显是受中文"当名人们出现在报纸上"的影响来翻译的。地道的用法是 when they **are exposed in** the news。

③ actions：行为，所做之事（具体）。此处用显得太"小"了，可以考虑用 behavior。

④ the standard of satisfaction：满意的标准。这个搭配比较奇怪。本句意思说"满意的标准飞速发展，因此完美更容易达到，大家也更期待"，这句话逻辑有问题，如果满意的标准增长快的话，人们应该不容易满足才对。放在这里，与上下文不搭界，句子间"咬"得不紧，这属于 SAT 忌讳的现象，建议删去本句。

⑤ disguise themselves from who they really are：可简化为 disguise their true selves。

⑥ in order to gain acceptance：不符合事实。作为名人，需要的不是赢得大家的接受（gain acceptance），而是维系已经获得的知名度，改为"in order to maintain popularity"。

⑦ in public gazes：改成 in spotlight 更地道。

<u>Back in 2004, Liu Xiang won the gold medal of men's 110m huddle with a record-breaking time in the Olympics⑧</u>; he became a superstar and many Chinese awaited him to <u>retain the glory⑨</u> <u>on the home front⑩</u>. <u>Quite ironically⑪</u>, Xiang had not yet recovered from his injury, and he walked off the track just before the qualifier started. Because of Xiang's popularity, an otherwise perfectly common situation-an athlete quits a race due to injury-ignited a great debate nationwide; more shockingly, <u>many furious people attacked Xiang's character⑫</u>, which caused great controversies on the Internet. One who achieved the most notable glory for his

country was maliciously degraded[13]; <u>one of the reasons is we expect too much from</u> <u>him</u>[14]. We expect Xiang to run despite of his injuries when we ourselves could not have done so.

⑧ 本句的 back in 2004 与句尾的 in the Olympics 距离太远。另外,"打破纪录"和"获得金牌"应该用两个连续动词,而不是使用非常拗口的"record-breaking time"。本句可改为:Back in 2004 Olympics, Liu Xiang broke the record of men's 110m huddle and won the gold medal.

⑨ retain the glory:作者本意指"再创辉煌",但受母语影响,出现了这样奇怪的搭配。可使用 create another wonder, scale new heights 等等。

⑩ home front:作者本意指主场比赛,最好用 Beijing 2008 Olympics。

⑪ Quite ironically:具有讽刺意味的是。用在此处不符合意思,有讥笑之嫌,而一个过于 cynical 的作者是令考官非常不快的。应该使用 Unfortunately 或者 To many people's disappointment。

⑫ many furious people attacked Xiang's character:可改为 many people even attacked Xiang's character,作者对于这些攻击谩骂者持不赞成态度,可加 even 一词。

⑬ degraded:堕落,道德沦丧,给人的感觉是刘翔已经堕落了,不合作者的本意,应该用 belittled 或 disparaged(贬低)。

⑭ 此句是表语从句,be 动词后面必须有 that。改为:one of the reasons is **that** we expect too much from him。注意,也有很多同学说 one of the reasons is because ... 也是不对的,必须要用 that。

The Beetles, one of the most loved bands in the world, has also been through bitter <u>criticizes</u>[15] when fans complained that they did not sing live in their MTV. <u>Anyone who sings</u>[16] knows how hard it is to <u>keep the breath right</u>[17], to follow the rhythm, to memorize the lyrics, as well as to express the right emotions[18]. Nevertheless, people chose to attack Beetles when they pre-recorded their song and lip-synched when acting for the music video. As time passes by, however, lip synching is gradually accepted by <u>public</u>[19] as they <u>found</u>[20] out that it is <u>almost</u> <u>impossible</u>[21] to dance and sing and act perfectly at the same time.

⑮ criticizes 是动词,此处应用名词 criticism。

⑯ Anyone who sings:最好改为 anyone who has a basic understanding of singing,更符合常理。

⑰ keep the breath right:control one's breath,与后面的 to follow the rhythm, to memorize the lyrics 结构上更平衡。

⑱ 此处缺少一个 simultaneously。

⑲ public：公众是 the public，此处少了个 the。

⑳ found：时态错，应为 find。

㉑ impossible：建议改为 almost unattainable 或 way too demanding。

Fame, by its nature, becomes the reason why people set much higher expectations for public figures㉒. Indeed㉓, we tend to ignore the fact㉔ that a sports superstar may have very bad taste, or a great singer may be reclusive and unwilling to talk㉕. The Beetles' lip synching and Xiang's withdrawal from the race reveal how the public are disappointed by the "cruel" reality, which is far different from their self-built image㉖. All men have their fortes and their flaws, including thriving stars and powerful leaders㉗; before we place our expectations on others, it is usually good to test them on ourselves. ㉘(**447 words**)

㉒ 结尾段应总结例子，复述中心思想；这种下定义句式太强调 fame 了。可以改为：We harbor(entertain) higher expectation for public figures just because we take it for granted that famous people are impeccable(完美无缺的)。同时，原句容易产生歧义，让人误解我们之所以对名人要求过多，是因为我们自己想获得 fame。另外，harbor(怀有)的用法很地道。

㉓ Indeed：此处应该使用转折连词，如 However 或 Yet 等等。

㉔ the fact：改成 the basic fact，强调"名人也是人"的普遍适用性。

㉕ 结尾段不应该再出现这么具体的句子，而应该抽象点，普遍点。可以改为：they are liable to make mistakes just like us；或 they are subject to fault just like us。另外，即使要具体，也要在具体的内容前加上点 general 的内容。

㉖ self-built image 没有这样的搭配。显然，中式思维再次作祟，可使用 public image。

㉗ thriving star and powerful leaders：最好改为 flamboyant stars and charismatic leaders，即光彩夺目的明星和充满个人魅力的领导。这样改的目的是因为在我们普通人看来是 flamboyant 和 charismatic 的名人，他们都是有缺点的。

㉘ 最后一句写得很棒，作为结束语，非常有启发性。

【文章分析】

"追星"现象不分国界。本文也正是针对这一现象进行分析。文章观点鲜明——光环下面,其实明星也是普通人,也有各种毛病。所举的例子非常好,刘翔与 Beatles,涵盖了文体界,横跨东西方,比较有代表性。

但是,文章也有比较明显的缺点。比如说,第一段逻辑关系不清楚,句子之间咬得不紧;第二段出现了若干个用词不够恰当的地方(quite ironically, degrade 等);另外,部分句子的中式思维痕迹比较明显。但瑕不掩瑜,整体上看,结构符合 SAT 作文要求,举例也很恰当,例子和中心论点间的关系也很紧密,如果撇开一些表达上的小问题,应该是 5 分以上的作文。

第二篇　人生最大的悲剧是自作自受

Think carefully about the issue presented in the following excerpt and the assignment below.

> "The greatest grieves are those we cause ourselves."
>
> — Sophocles

Assignment：What do you think of the view that the worst sorrows are those for which we are responsible? Plan and write an essay in which you develop your point of view on this issue. Support your position with reasoning and examples taken from your reading, studies, experience, or observations.

【学生原作】

In our present world, most of our sorrows are caused by none other than us.① There are many problematic environmental issues② and references of historical fictions in our present time③ that serve as examples of grieve precipitated④ by us.

① in our present world 表达成 in the modern world 更好，用 none other than 来强调 us 值得学习。

② problematic environmental issues：不简练，可改为 environmental problems。

③ in our present time：前面已经讲过"在当今时代"，此处可删去。

④ precipitated：这个单词的内在含意是"突然引起"，用在此处词义不贴切。

Recently, global warming has caused Earth's temperature to rise⑤ and result in a chain of other reactions, such as the loss of many Polar Bears in the Arctic and the collapsing colonies of the bees⑥ in the United States. The reasons for such tragedies originate from⑦ our abundant⑧ use of cars and other luxuries we take for granted. In addition, not only are many animals becoming extinct, but non-renewable resources such as fossil fuel are also being used up⑨ at an alarming rate.

⑤ global warming 本来就是 Earth's temperature to rise，这不存在谁引起谁的

逻辑关系。

⑥ Such as A and B：这种结构中，A 与 B 应该要平行。这里，A 是 the loss of many Polar Bears，B 是 the collapsing colonies of the bees，一个是抽象名词 loss，一个是具体名词 colonies of bees，不平行。可改为：such as the death of many Polar Bears and the collapse of bees' colonies，这样等于是两个抽象名词 death 和 collapse 平行，很完美。

⑦ 表达"某某现象后面是什么原因"，固定的句型："The reasons for … （现象） stem from … （原因）"。（stem from：源于，某事由……导致；originate from：起源于，如：All theories originate from practice and in turn serve practice. ）

⑧ abundant：大量的，有褒义，此处可使用 excessive 这样的中性词。

⑨ used up：这样使用没有问题，但为什么不用 deplete /exhaust resources 这样更符合正式文风的单词呢？

There are⑩ also themes in fiction such as the story of Romeo and Juliet which exemplifies this concept. For instance, it is only after the death of Romeo and Joliet do both Old Montague and Old Capulet realize that their bloody feud had caused their child's death along with the death of many others. If the two families had never hated each other to begin with, Romeo and Juliet would have lived. This story reflects many of the issues in the world today, in places where hatred is common. ⑪

(**212 words**)

⑩ There are 这样的句式毫无新奇之处，不建议使用，可以删去。此处作为段落开始，可以使用衔接句子。比如：Another example is the story of Romeo and Juliet ，which also exemplifies this concept.

⑪ 讲完例子后，此处应针对例子再发表感想，而不是泛泛地谈世界上仇恨泛滥。此处可改为：Unfortunately，however，hatred ran through their vein and stripped off their sound reasoning and finally ruined the two otherwise happy families.

Sorrows in which we cause ourselves⑫ are interminable as long as our avarice and hate continues⑬ to pushes⑭ us to seek unneeded luxury and violence⑮.

⑫ 介词用得不准确。应改为：Sorrows which we cause to ourselves。

⑬ continues：主语为 avarice 和 hate，谓语用复数 continue。

⑭ pushes：不定式后带原形 push。

⑮ 作为结尾段，任务可一点也不轻松，要重复观点，精练地回顾例子，最后再

展望及发表感想。而我们这里的结尾，充其量只完成了最后一个任务，因此需要扩充。

【文章分析】

本文只有两百多词，明显偏少。

本文第二段举全球变暖造成的生物种类灭绝的例子，第三段举 Romeo and Juliet 的例子，两个例子都很好，与中心思想契合，但例证展开不充分，文章缺乏洋洋洒洒的气势，也不那么有说服力。

怎样展开例证呢？

比如在这篇文章里，我们可以在讲完一个例子后，加入自己的感想。如果还嫌不够，可以在文章结尾段再来点感想，都不为过。

另外，本文的文笔欠流畅，句子结构也不够丰富。比如第二段 abundant use of cars 说明对词语的褒义贬义还不很清楚；第一段和第三段开头的 there be 句型说明作者还习惯使用简单的句型。

第三篇　我们从成功还是从失败中学到的更多

Think carefully about the issue presented in the following excerpt and the
assignment below.

> Man should never be ashamed to own he has been in the wrong, which is
> but saying, in other words, that he is wiser today than he was yesterday.
>
> *Alexander Pope*

Assignment：Do we learn more from finding out that we have made mistakes or
from our successful actions? Plan and write an essay in which you
develop your point of view on this issue. Support your position
with reasoning and examples taken from your reading, studies,
experience, or observations.

【学生原作】

People sometimes <u>are shamed about</u>① their <u>past — the mistakes they have
made</u>②. However, without our past, our future would be a tortuous path leading to
nowhere. In order to move up the ladder of success and achievement, we must come
to terms with our past and integrate it into our future. Even if <u>in the past</u>③ we made
mistakes, this will only make wiser people out of us and guide us to where we are
supposed to be. From Rod Johnson to world's popular Internet search engine,
Google Inc., the lesson is the same：<u>We learn from mistakes, they</u>④ help us
understand and appreciate success.

① 没有 be shamed about 这个搭配,应改为 be ashamed of：以为……是耻辱。

② past — the mistakes they have made：破折号往往代表解释,但这里需要的
明显不是解释,而是表原因的连接。可改为：past because of the mistakes they
have made。

③ 受中式思维"尽管我们过去犯错误"的影响。其实,made 已经暗含"过去",
再加个 in the past 就多余了,就如 in the future will do something 中的 in the future
也是多余的,因为 will 就是表示未来了。

④ 这属于串句中的 comma split，可以改为：We learn from mistakes, which . . . 。

The success of Rod Johnson as <u>an entrepreneur in the recruiting field</u> [5] shows how effective learning from mistakes and failure can be. Rather than accept his failure after being laid off, Johnson decided to study <u>it</u> [6]. After a month of research, he realized that his failure to find a new job resulted primarily from the inefficiency of the local job placement agencies, not from his own deficiencies. A month later, Johnson <u>created</u> [7] Johnson Staffing to <u>correct this weakness</u>[8] in the job placement sector. <u>As Johnson Staffing is becoming</u>[9] the largest job placement agency in <u>South American market</u>[10], it is also in the process of expanding into a national corporation.

⑤ an entrepreneur in the recruiting field 太泛，可改为 a job replacement agency。

⑥ it 指代不明，到底是要 study 什么呢？

⑦ created 改为 founded（成立，创立）更地道，create 是"创造"。

⑧ correct this weakness 搭配牵强，可改为 address this weakness。

⑨ As Johnson Staffing is becoming 中的 as 到底指时间还是指原因不清楚。本句可改为：Johnson Staffing is now the largest job placement agency in Southern America, with an aim of expanding into a multinational corporation.

⑩ South American 有歧义。是指南美洲还是美国南部呢？按字面指南美洲，结合文意，改为 Southern America。

Another example of a success achieved by studying from earlier failures is the [11] Internet search engine company, Google Inc., which <u>has suffered</u>[12] few setbacks since it went into business in the late 1990s. Google has succeeded by studying the failures of other companies in order to help it innovate its technology and business model. ____ [13] Google identified and solved the problem of assessing the quality of search results by using the number of links pointing to a page as an indicator of the number of people who find the page valuable. Surprisingly, Google's search results became far more accurate and reliable than those from other companies, and now <u>Google's dominance in the field of Internet search is almost absolute</u>[14].

⑪ 少一个 leading。

⑫ has suffered：suffer 词义色彩为贬义，此处用中性的为佳，可以用 experienced。

⑬ 此处欠缺交代，其他提供搜索引擎的公司遭遇到了怎样的失败？可以补充：The quality of searching results has long been a bottleneck for many companies, and no breakthrough has been made until Google was set up.

⑭ 中式表达。可改为：Google enjoys absolute dominance in the field of Internet search engine.

Mistakes are often seen as embarrassing, something to be denied and hidden⑮. But as the examples of Rod Johnson and Google Inc. prove, if an individual, or an organization⑯ is strong enough to face and study mistakes in the past ____⑰, then those mistakes can become a powerful teacher⑱.

⑮ hidden 是自己躲藏，而 covered 是人为故意藏起来，此处用 covered。

⑯ an organization 后要有逗号，否则为 run-on 串句。

⑰ 文章中说 Google 公司从其他公司错误中吸取教训，自己几乎无错，因此这里要把情况讲全面点，可以加一个 or learn from other's mistakes。

⑱ become 用得不地道，act as a wise teacher 更好。

【文章分析】

文章第一段有抄袭 collegeboard 范文的痕迹，乃 SAT 大忌。哪怕你能把范文背下来用在你的文章中，也是抄袭。这一点，希望各位考生千万要注意。

文章还有另外一个重大问题，就是例子不太切合观点。比如说，文章的 assignment 中问"Do we learn more from finding out what we have made mistakes or from our successful actions?"即"我们从**我们的**错误还是**我们的**成功中学得更多呢？"这篇文章第二个例子举 google 公司，文章中说"自从它成立后，顺风顺水，因为它从**其他公司的**错误中总结很多"。这就是一个不贴切的例子。因为**不是自己的错误让自己进步，而是从其他公司的错误中吸取经验教训让自己进步**。这个问题，考官糊涂状态下不容易看出，但……还是让我们祈祷他正好下午一点半看到这篇文章吧，正是打瞌睡的时候。

第四篇　面对危机，应该快速反应还是慎重考虑

Think carefully about the issue presented in the following excerpt and the assignment below.

> A man who waits to believe in action before acting is anything you like, but he is not a man of action. It is as if a tennis player before returning the ball stopped to think about his views of the physical and mental advantages of tennis. You must act as you breathe.
>
> *Georges Clemenceau*

Assignment：Is it true that acting quickly and instinctively is the best response to a crisis? Or are there times when an urgent situation requires a more careful consideration and a slower response? Plan and write an essay in which you develop your point of view on this issue. Support your position with reasoning and examples taken from your reading, studies, experience, or observations.

【学生原作】

Due to the technology① development, the world becomes② a global village. Within this close distance③, nations can be greatly impacted by others' movement④. Likewise⑤, all the impacts transform from local to international and from mild to intense⑥. Therefore⑦, the best response to a crisis is to act immediately and instinctively. As the examples of the recent Economic Crisis and Hitler's aggressive invasion in World War Ⅱ⑧, any urgent situation requires a quick response.

① technology 要改成形容词形 technological。

② becomes 改为 has become，因为现在的世界已经是个地球村了。

③ Within this close distance：世界变成地球村，但 distance 还是一点没有变。我们可以换更普通的说法：coinciding with this change。

④ nations can be greatly impacted by others' movement：movement 一词比较含糊，我们可以把句子重点意思放在动词上可改为：One nation can be influenced heavily by each other。

⑤ Likewise：类似的。这里并不存在具有可比性的变化，所以应该使用层进关系的连词，比如 Furthermore，In addition。

⑥ transform from local to international and from mild to intense：这里的关系太挤，我们可以展开说，比如：The changes take place from local scale to international scale，and the impacts gradually evolve from mild ones to intense ones.

⑦ Therefore 这里缺少一个过渡。可以在 Therefore 前加一个句子 The urgency of the problem leaves us no time to give these issues a second thought。

⑧ 缺少动词，"As XXX demonstrates，..."。另外使用 financial storm /turmoil (金融危机)更好。原文可改为：As the examples of the recent financial storm and Hitler's aggressive invasion in World War II demonstrate。

When the Lehman Brothers Holding collapsed，a huge chain of economy crisis started secretly. However，American government <u>did not realize</u>⑨ how this was going to <u>impact the world's economy immediately and heavily</u>⑩. Not only a huge number of Americans become unemployed and their lifetime savings <u>disappeared</u>⑪, but also other big companies and banks like AIG and Citibank almost <u>bankrupted</u>⑫. American government's slow response to the collapse of Wall Street companies <u>leads the world into a huge global stagnant economy</u>⑬. Although there is no quick <u>solution to solve</u>⑭ the downturn economy，this <u>experience</u>⑮ teaches every countries that any crisis should be dealt instantly and <u>even to</u>⑯ the foreshadowing of catastrophe should be handled instinctively.

⑨ did not realize 是个客观陈述，应该有一个暗含作者态度的句子。此处可改为 failed to realize 或 was too slow to realize。

⑩ immediately and heavily：某事如何**迅速而深入地**影响全球经济。这个搭配确实有点牵强。可以把 impact sth. immediately and heavily 改为 make a strong impact on，或更高级点的 exert adverse and instant impact on。

⑪ disappear 这个词过于简单，可用 evaporate 替代。

⑫ bankrupt 一般与 go 搭配，此处可改为 went bankrupt。

⑬ 改成 finally caused global stagnant economy。

⑭ solution to solve 意思重复，应去掉 solve。同时，应该是 solution to

doing sth.。

⑮ experience 为中性词，无法表达作者态度，可改为 tragedy。

⑯ even to 在这里强调的是一种多余的递进关系。同时，从文法角度看，and 前面找不到可以和 to 并列的介词，to 后面的句子意思也很模糊，所以删去 even to 带的分句。

The cause of World War II is another crisis brought up by slow response. ⑰ In 1938，Hitler made series of aggressive invasions toward⑱ the neighbour countries⑲. Notwithstanding, the strong European countries were reluctant to punish his invasion. The year after 1938，Germany took over the rest of Czechoslovakia and invaded Poland. Then, in the same year, Britain and France declared war on Germany and World War II began. ⑳ This history teaches us that any negligence may lead to unfortunate results that can never be solved or repaired. Therefore, all the nations must act immediately to others' harmful movement especially in this global world㉑.

⑰ 二战的原因怎么能是反应慢带来的灾难呢？逻辑上说，二战才是反应慢带来的灾难。可以改为 World War II is another example of how slow response directly leads to crisis。

⑱ invasions 后面带介词 into 或者 on。

⑲ the neighbour countries 应改为 the neighbouring countries。

⑳ 这句话太轻描淡写了，全然没有责备英国、法国应战德国速度过慢的意思，导致这段到底要批评谁、反对谁，关系不清楚。可以改为 It was not until then that Britain and France declared war on Germany, a time when every possible means of stopping the Nazis was futile, making the World War II an inevitable occurrence。

㉑ harmful movement：搭配不地道。而且也把要快速反应的范围大大缩小了——好像只需要在对方有 harmful movement 的时候才有必要似的。本句可改为 all nations must act immediately, especially in terms of the national defence。

Surely, a response to an urgent situation requires more considerations. Nevertheless, the recent Economic Crisis and Hitler's aggressive invasions demonstrate two negative results㉒ of slow response. Therefore, a crisis should be responded instantaneously㉓ since any irreparable changes could happen within the consideration time㉔. (**332 words**)

㉒ demonstrate two negative results：是"显示负面的结果"的中式翻译，可改为 are two examples showing the dire consequences。

㉓ 被动语态，用在此处过于文气。可改为 We should respond instantaneously。

㉔ "考虑时间"翻译成 the consideration time，又是受母语影响，不地道。改成 with no time for consideration 或 in a flash。

【文章分析】

本文的例子本身比较典型，也切合题目中心思想。但是故事叙述得不生动，例子与论点的逻辑关系也不强。

比如说，在讲二战德国例子时，应该说出这样的一句话来把例子与观点"钩"住：德国入侵周边国家时，欧洲强国应该做出快速反应来制止这种侵略，但他们没有这么做，所以导致德国长驱直入。这种只讲故事不评述的方式，只会弱化文章的观点，让读者不知所云。

第五篇 说谎还是说出事实真相
（学生习作之一）

Think carefully about the issue presented in the following excerpt and the assignment below.

> A little inaccuracy saves a world of explanation.
>
> *C. E. Ayers*

Assignment: Is it always essential to tell the truth, or are there circumstances in which it is better to lie? Plan and write an essay in which you develop your point of view on this issue. Support your position with reasoning and examples taken from your reading, studies, experience, or observations.

【学生原作】

World [①] is not actually as beautiful as we imagine. It's full of setbacks, barriers and darkness. Always [②], truth is a dagger, hurts our hearts, truth is the most brutal beast, makes us nowhere to hide. [③] Perhaps, lies are kinder and gentler, although they're not true, they still have the magic to convince us to go straight ahead, to have belief that everything is going to be better [④].

① 联系第二句，我们知道作者其实表达的是 life is full of setbacks, barriers and darkness，所以这里应该用 Life。

② Always：过于绝对的语言，尽量避免，可换成 in many senses 或 in many cases 等。

③ 结构有问题，可以使用动名词结构进行优化。可改成 truth is a dagger, hurting our hearts 或 truth is the most brutal beast, leaving us nowhere to hide。

④ 本句有比较大的问题，也是考生经常会出现的问题——想表现出思维的成熟，使用过多绕来绕去的词，却最终显得犹犹豫豫，思维混乱。这句话其实应该快刀斩乱麻，改为 However, lies are magic, giving us hopes of going straight forward, and convincing us that everything is going to be better。lies are kinder and gentler

的表达都是很不地道的,也影响了句子核心意思的展示。

It's a real story happened on a desert⑤. Two explorers lost their direction, unfortunately⑥, their water couldn't afford them⑦ more than 3 days, water meant life on a desert, these two explorers felt death was walking towards them⑧. However⑨, one day, one of the explorers took out one bottle of water, he⑩ said he prepared⑪ it for emergency before they started the trip. But⑫ they could only drink it after they got the destination safely. Because of this bottle of water⑬, these two explorers picked up the hope and belief again, finally they got out of the predicament⑭. But⑮ when they opened the bottle, they found⑯ it was just a bottle of sands. What a beautiful lie it was! If one of the explorers didn't lie, he and his partner probably would lose the power to face up this challenge, and even give up the chance to live⑰. The lie let them found the direction and alive⑱.

⑤ 应改为 which happened 或 happening, happened 是 which is(was)的省略形式。on a desert 应该是 in a desert。

⑥ 应改为 to make things worse 更能表达效果,另外,要在这个词组前加上 and,不然和前面的句子构成了不间断句子。

⑦ 应该是 sustain them,或直接说 last。

⑧ 首先要把 water meant life 前面的逗号改为句号,water 变为大写,这样本句和前面的句子就不 run-on 了。同时 these two explorers 前面加上连词 so。walking towards them 改成 approaching 更正式,或者说 felt death was imminent(即将到来的)。

⑨ 此处并没有强烈的转折,不需要 however。

⑩ 此处 water 可以加一个双引号表示特指,并且此句出现串句,应改为"water", and he said 或者"water", saying。

⑪ prepared 在这里表示之前的之前,应该用过去完成时,加一个 had。

⑫ 这个聪明的 traveller 话没有讲完,这里 But 应小写,句子变成分句归到前面去,同时把 trip 后的句号改为逗号。

⑬ water 应加引号表特指。

⑭ 又串句了! 应改为 **and** finally they got out of the predicament。

⑮ 此处故事讲完,情节达到高潮,但需要一个长点的词组来代替"when"稍微缓冲下。可改为 Once arriving at the destination, they couldn't wait to open the bottle,以此来表达当时他们迫不及待要喝水的心情。

⑯ they found 太平铺直叙了，用 only to find 代替，有惊讶之意。在逗号后的 only to do something 常常表示一个意想不到的或不愉快的结果。如：We hurried to the bus stop, only to find that the bus had just left.

⑰ 此处应该使用虚拟语气，表示和过去情况相反，应该改为 If one of the explorers had not lied, he and his partner would probably have lost the power to face up this challenge, and even would have given up the chance to live.

⑱ let 后面要用动词原形 find 做宾语补足语；and 前后结构要平行，加个动词 come back。本句改为 The lie let them find the direction and come back alive。

Another real story happened in Sichuan，China. On May 12th, 2008, a devastating earthquake <u>had taken away so many lives</u>⑲. <u>A 5-year-old boy lost his father, he cried everyday, kept asking his mother where his father had gone</u> ⑳. The mother pretended everything was fine, <u>she told her son,"Don't worry, dear, your father is doing well, he's helping others go through this nightmare, he is our pride, don't worry, he will come back definitely</u> ㉑." ____ ㉒ When other kids were crying for their lost parents, this little boy didn't weep at all,<u>he behaved so mature and brave,</u>㉓<u>he</u>㉔ told the journalist he wouldn't cry because he would <u>wait for his father coming back</u> ㉕, <u>he wanted to</u> ㉖ behave like a man in order to get the laud from his father. I don't know if the boy <u>gets the truth</u>㉗ now, but at that moment, it was his mother's lie that gave him courage to go through this catastrophe, <u>his little heart and his hero</u>㉘ was protected <u>without any ruins</u>㉙ by this <u>kind lie</u>㉚.

⑲ had taken away so many lives：用过去时就可以了，so many 也过于泛，可改为 took away thousands of lives。

⑳ 两次出现串句现象，使用从句纠正，改为 A 5-year-old boy who lost his father cried everyday and kept asking his mother where his father had gone.

㉑ 串句！改为 telling his son. 引号里面的一大堆不间断句子，但由于是引用别人说话，所以就不做修改了。

㉒ 要来一句衔接语。After hearing this, the boy breathed a sign of relief.

㉓ 串句！改为 behaving maturely and bravely。

㉔ 串句！改为 He，前一个逗号改为句号。

㉕ wait for his father coming back：应该改为 wait for his father to come back。

㉖ 串句！改为 and he must。

㉗ gets the truth 的 get 过于口语化，改为 has known the real story。

㉘ his little heart and his hero：他的英雄到底是谁指代不清楚。可改为 his little heart and his soul，同时在 his little ... 前加 and 以避免不间断句子错误。

㉙ without any ruins：改为 without being bruised 更地道。

㉚ kind lie 不如 white lie（善意的谎言）更地道。

In fact, lie sometimes is more beautiful than the truth in certain circumstances. It makes us believe in unreal scenes , it ㉛ makes us believe there're still hopes in our miserable life, no matter how ridiculous the lie is, no matter how illusory the lie is㉜. Although it's somewhat ironic to depend on a lie㉝ , I still value it, I still consider it more precious than emotionless truth ㉞.

㉛ 串句，需要在 it 前加 and 或者把 it 前的逗号改成分号。

㉜ 串句，并且太不紧凑，把两句合并起来，改为 no matter how ridiculous or illusory the lie is。

㉝ depend on a lie 改成 believe in a lie；ironic 改为 ridiculous 更合适。

㉞ emotionless truth：不露感情的事实，这个搭配不地道，此处用"无情的现实"更贴切，可换成 merciless fact 或 cruel reality。

【文章分析】

文章所举例子，不仅贴切，而且感性，令人动容。

第一个是寓言故事，沙漠里两位旅行者，凭借着一瓶装着沙子的"水"，走出了绝地。第二个是汶川大地震中，等待父亲归来的男孩的故事。

例子贴切，叙述流畅，笔风细腻。但是，倘若要评"最顽固错误文章"，本篇当之无愧！串句现象层出不穷，一段话用一个句子就说完了！

叙述时，我们常常会出现写小说的冲动，以至于根本就不管标点符号，先写过瘾再说。但是，我们现在面对的是以评判式思维见长的 SAT 考官，而不是感情丰沛的好莱坞导演，所以我们必须收起情感化的流畅，考虑文字标点问题。小小举动，将使考生受益无穷。

第六篇　说谎还是说出事实真相
（学生习作之二）

Think carefully about the issue presented in the following excerpt and the assignment below.

> A little inaccuracy saves a world of explanation.
>
> *C. E. Ayers*

Assignment：Is it always essential to tell the truth, or are there circumstances in which it is better to lie? Plan and write an essay in which you develop your point of view on this issue. Support your position with reasoning and examples taken from your reading, studies, experience, or observations.

【学生原作】

For centuries① we have been taught by teachers and parents to always tell the truth, and that telling the truth is never wrong. Although in many cases, the truth is the best answer, lies are sometimes necessary②.

① For centuries：这个词组不符合事实，让人感觉 we 好像能活几个世纪一样。若 we 代表所有人，那么 centuries 表达的时间概念又短了点，不如直接删掉好了。

② something is the best answer /policy 这种用法非常地道，但这里应该再多讲两句话，两句一段做开头还是少了点。

In the case of the American Civil War, many slaves traveled the Underground Railroad to escape their tortuous lives③. Along the way, many freed slaves and even white Americans assisted these run-always by providing food, shelter, and most importantly, by lying to slave catchers about the hiding places or trails of the slaves. Their lies often led catchers to wrong directions, buying time for the slaves. ④ By lying, these helpers saved and freed many lives. Without the help from those freed people⑤, many salves would have been easily caught by the slave catchers, who are ⑥ equipped with guns and dogs. Once caught, these slaves ____ ⑦ face cruel punishment or even death⑧. Although the helpers lied to slave owners and catchers, they helped end the horrifying lives of many slaves⑨ and led America closer to racial equality⑩.

③ travel 这个词色彩中性,用在这里感情不够;tortuous 这个词意思是"弯曲的","含混不清的",不能用在这里(作者可能想用的是 torturous)。可改为 escaped their torturous lives via the Underground Railroad。

④ buy time for something 的用法很地道,意思是"为某事争取了时间"。

⑤ Without the help from those freed people:不精练,改为 Without their help。

⑥ 应该是 were。

⑦ 少用了 would,本句是个虚拟语气句。

⑧ death 也有可能是正常死亡,在此处明显是死刑的意思,应改为 death penalty。

⑨ 重大歧义。helped end the horrifying lives of many slaves 中 end one's life 可以理解为"杀死某人",可改为 helped many slaves to escape their horrifying lives。

⑩ led America closer to racial equality:前后语义有因果关系,此处应加一个 hence /therefore /as a result /consequently 进行过渡。另外 closer 不地道,可改为 consequently led America a step farther in racial equality。

In literature, too, many authors benefitted from lying about themselves. The Bronte sisters, who are famous for their great literature⑪, published their works under male names. They wrote at a time when women only washed clothes and cooked foods for their husbands. ⑫ The Bronte sisters had no hopes of publishing their novels in such a male dominated society if they had used their real names. ⑬ By publishing under different names, the sisters' novels were widely accepted and critically acclaimed⑭. The Bronte sisters demonstrated that lying can be essential at times as their own works would have never been published had they not adopted male names.

⑪ literature 这个词太大,可改为 literature endowment /talent /accomplishment。

⑫ only 是为了表示妇女们仅干低等活,但它使读者误认为妇女只干这两个活。可改为 women were characterized as one only suitable to do laundry and cooking 或者 women's sole job was confined to doing laundry and cooking。

⑬ 这句话结构不清楚,应该把状语放在句首,if 从句用介词短语结构代替,可改为: In such a male dominated society, the Bronte sisters had no hopes of publishing their novels under real names。

⑭ 两个平行词组很优美。

Many times，telling the truth is usually better than <u>telling a lie，however</u>⑮ in the case of helping the escaped slaves in the American Civil War and the Bronte sisters，lying proved necessary. Lies helped many slaves <u>obtain free and safe lives</u>⑯ , and allowed the Bronte sisters to <u>show their works of literature</u>⑰. <u>These are only two examples which show lying can be beneficial and sometimes essential</u>⑱.（**344 words**）

⑮ 前面都是 telling lies，这里就不能使用 telling a lie，以免产生歧义。另外，however 不是连词，所以在 however 前要加个分号。

⑯ 获得自由和安全的生活，翻译成 obtain free and safe lives 是因为中式思维的干扰，可改为 obtain freedom and safety。

⑰ 展示文学作品，翻译成 show their works of literature，也是中式思维；另外，works of literature 不自然，拗口，改为 publish their literature works。

⑱ 行文至此，戛然而止，总觉得少了点什么，应该再来句感想。比如：Suppose that they had never told a lie，how many lives would have lost and how regretful we would have lost an illustrious name in literature world!

【文章分析】

本文举的是美国内战时期，自由人在帮助黑人奴隶逃跑时经常"说谎"蒙骗追逐者的事例；第二个例子是勃朗特姐妹在男权社会里，不得不使用男性笔名来发表作品，也算是"谎言"。

作者赢在观点新颖，例证合理。因为通常在论证"诚实还是说谎"的是非时，一般比较容易偏向诚实，而本文反其道而行之，论证有力，结合的又都是英国、美国历史上比较典型的事例，非常到位。

第七篇　改变自身态度还是改变环境
（8分真题作文）

Think carefully about the issue presented in the following excerpt and the assignment below.

> If we are dissatisfied with our circumstances, we think about changing them. But the most important and effective changes — in our attitude — hardly occur to us. In other words, we should worry not about how to alter the world around us for the better but about how to change ourselves in order to fit into that world.
>
> Adapted from Michael Hymers, "*Wittgenstein, Pessimism and Politics*"

Assignment： Is it better to change one's attitude than to change one's circumstances? Plan and write an essay in which you develop your point of view on this issue. Support your position with reasoning and examples taken from your reading, studies, experience, or observations.

【学生原作】

_____ ① I think this② completely depends on what type of circumstances.

_____ ③If you live in a place where you are subject to a despotic ruler, changing your attitude does not help because the ruler will continue to mistreat his citizens. For example, if the French people did not rebel in 1799, many more people will starve to death for an extended period of time. If Martin Luther King adapted his attitude in line with the rest, African Americans might still face segregation and discrimination. Therefore, sometimes④ , conformists contribute to the aggressiveness of the oppressor. By conforming to the oppressors, it will make them think they have all the power in the world to do whatever they are doing to the powerless and vulnerable people.

① 把提示中的观点加上去，让文章的开头完整。Michael Hymers believed

that "we should worry not about how to alter the world around us for the better but about how to change ourselves in order to fit into that world". Is this always the case? I don't think so.

② this 指代不明，本句可改为：Whether to yield to the circumstances completely depends on。另外，尽量不要用 I think 之类的语句，因为你的态度已经包含在句子里了，再使用 I think 会显得文风稚嫩。

③ 此处应该分段，并且在段首加上"on the one hand"，与下一段开头"on the other hand"呼应，对比意味更明显。

④ sometimes 放在这里意义不清楚，结构上也不漂亮，删去。

On the other hand, <u>there are many people who think the world should revolve around them</u>[5]. They attempt to change everything to meet their expectations _____[6]. These people <u>usually craving</u>[7] power over everything and everybody. They always want control and <u>it</u>[8] could turn deviant. <u>Project the thought farther, the earlier stage is about simple satisfaction of gaining power, but later, these people can become aggressive as they gain new powers</u>[9]. For instance, the terrorists who are politically motivated, like the one in Northern Ireland, <u>they</u>[10] want independence from the United Kingdom; in order to accomplish their mission of independence they employ series of terror tactics to harm ordinary people for their own political interests. I think these are the people who need to be brought in line with the general public; otherwise they will continue to cause bloodshed to innocent people. (**263 words**)

⑤ 要尽量避免 there be 句型。另外，作者批驳的行为"想让世界围着我转"(people who think the world should revolve around them)又有什么毛病呢？为了使其在逻辑上更易判断，我们把他们的想法"恶劣化"，句子改成：certain people would sacrifice others for the sole purpose of their own interests.

⑥ 同上理，为了行文清楚，逻辑分明，可加一句进行强调 even at the cost of others' lives.

⑦ usually 后面要用动词原形 crave。

⑧ it 指代不明，可用 this inclination 代替。

⑨ Project the thought farther 搭配很奇怪。整个句子大意是，这些权利欲望极强的人对于权利的攫取欲望是一步步增强的。这句话虽然看起来有 critical thinking 倾向，但与主题句不相关，可以删掉。

⑩ 此处的 they 多余，放在这里就出现了双主语的错误。

【文章分析】

文章只有区区两段，脑袋长到了躯干里，明显没有结尾，所以看起来，无头无尾，甚是奇怪。我们建议，第一句话要引用一下 promt 中的观点，加上作者自己的观点，使两个观点有对比，与例证分离出来，成为开头段。

在文章结尾，加一个光荣的尾巴，凑成有开头有结尾的完整四段式文章。但本文最大的问题还不是无头无尾，而是观点不清晰。

第一个例子讲的是，有的人不与环境妥协，终于带来社会进步，比如法国 1799 年革命和美国民权运动领导人马丁·路德·金；第二个例子讲的是，有的人一味以自己意志为中心，为达成目的不择手段，给身边的民众带来灾难，并以北爱尔兰的恐怖主义分子为例。

第一段，不要与环境妥协，革命比妥协好。

第二段，不要太以自我为中心，还是要妥协。

这不是自相矛盾吗？

也许作者的第一句就表明了他的态度：到底妥协还是不妥协，这要看这个环境。也许他想表达的意思是，倘若环境是独裁的政治，那么就不要妥协，去争取民主；倘若环境是民主的，那么就别折腾了，免得生灵涂炭，破坏和平。但是，这个论点非常容易被反驳，因为环境到底是民主还是独裁的，这个评判标准又如何定呢？难道是作者主观来定吗？暴徒与革命者往往只有一步之遥，作者到底又了解北爱尔兰的恐怖分子多少呢？

本文逻辑关系过于复杂，作者自乱阵脚。本文的题目是：Is it better to change one's attitude than to change one's circumstances? 这是一个简单的二选一观点题。作者可以在第一段阐述观点，要改变 circumstances，妥协无法带来社会进步；再把法国革命和美国民权运动两个例子阐述详细点，深刻点，各自作为一个自然段进行展开，就很棒了。

这是一篇真题作文，学生本身的英文功底和写作能力都是很不错的，之所以仅拿到 8 分，问题在于表述。说理性的东西太多了，整个文章很不活泼，写的内容也是别人不愿意看的东西，涉及政治和民主这样的一些比较抽象枯燥的话题，可以说整个作文的方向出了问题。但阅卷者还是看到了这个学生的功底，所以最后还是给了 8 分。笔者认为这 8 分应该有 2 分是对他写作功底的一种认可，如果仅仅从内容上看，恐怕连 8 分都危险。

读完整篇文章，可以感觉到作者迫切地想说些什么，但非常遗憾，他说的别人没有听懂。

第八篇　助人者自助（10分真题作文）

Think carefully about the issue presented in the following excerpt and the assignment：

> Why do people help others? Many philosophers and psychologists claim that everything people do, no matter how noble and beneficial to others, is really directed toward the ultimate goal of self-benefit. According to this view, helping others is always motivated by the prospect of some benefit to the helper, however small, and not out of genuine concern for the welfare of another.
>
> Adapted from C. Daniel Batson, *The Altruism Question*

Assignment：Do we only help others in order to help ourselves in some way? Plan and write an essay in which you develop your point of view on this issue. Support your position with reasoning and examples taken from your reading, studies, experience, or observations.

【学生原作】

Nobody is selfless①. Although many are magnanimous and are willing to help others, they do so, most of the time, seeking② something in return. When we lend a kind hand to others, we are in turn helping ourselves in someway; what we get "paid back" may not be something physical③ like money, but is definitely beneficial to ourselves, such as reputation, name or recognition. Throughout history and literature, we can clearly see that those who seem to be altruistic are instead, a little selfish④.

① 开篇第一句,提出没有人不自私,也就是说人人自私,这句话太绝对。

② seeking 改成 just to seek,不定式表示目的。

③ 这里想表达"我们要的也许不是金钱这样物质的东西",但是我们一般说物质(与钱相关)时,用 material 更好。

④ 这里的 a little 来得无理由,既然人人自私,凭什么断定这些利他主义者只

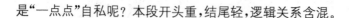

是"一点点"自私呢？本段开头重，结尾轻，逻辑关系含混。

In Mary Shelley's famous novel *Frankenstein*, the creature Frankenstein is one⑤ born innocent and kind. While he is in the woods alone, he perceives⑥ an indigent and miserable family and decides to help. Every morning, the monster collects woods for the family and during winters, he shovels snow for them. However, what appears to be free-giving and altruistic action has its intentions — Frankenstein seeks acceptance by the family. Since he is always disgusted and ostracized⑦ by the human society, the monster wants to earn companions. By "alleviating" the family's burden, the creature wishes that they will sincerely befriend with⑧ him. Nevertheless, Frankenstein's plan failed, as at the end the family does not recognize him⑨ for all the kind deeds he has done. The character Frankenstein proves to us that some people help others in an attempt to benefit themselves. Canada, as a nation, did something similar in history⑩.

⑤ 这个 one 删去更好，be born something 是一个惯常搭配结构。

⑥ perceive 是带观点、带态度地察觉，在这里使用 come across 就够了。

⑦ be ostracized(被流放)，用在这里太重，改为 isolated(被孤立的)。

⑧ befriend 是及物动词，以朋友的方式对待、照顾。这里不能出现介词 with。类似这样的后面直接带宾语的动词还有很多，比如：contact，marry，solute，希望大家多收集，并正确使用。不能说 solute to somebody，应该说 solute somebody。

⑨ at the end 应该是 in the end。

这里的 recognize 误用了，recognize 是"认识，认得"，这里应该是"接受或承认"的意思。按照文意应该是这一家人拒绝承认 Frankenstein 做的一切，拒绝接纳他。可改为 does not accept him in spite of his efforts。

⑩ 很明显，这句话应该放在下面一段，起到承上启下的作用。

During the First World War, Canada readily offered help to its mother country Britain. It joined the Allied and fought in the war alongside with Britain, France and U. S. Although Canada suffered great loses, it gained something in return — recognition as an independent country. Before the war, Canada was still under British Country⑪. _____⑫ By the end of the war, Canada signed the Paris Peace Treaty as an independent nation. It also gained its own seat at the League of Nations. Therefore, by aiding the Allied in the war, Canada helped itself in establishing its name[13].

⑪ under British Country 的意思含混不清，是指地位低下还是指受英国统治？明显是后者，所以可改为 under the rule of U. K.

⑫ 这里缺少一个转折词 However。

⑬ establishing its name：扬名。但这里还没有到扬名的地步，还只是成为一个独立的主权国家，应改为 establishing its status as an independent country。

The character Frankenstein, although fails[14], helps the family in an attempt to help himself extricate from[15] his state as a loner. Canada, too, helped British in World War One to earn world recognition as an independent country. Are the deeds they did for others beneficial? [16] Yes, they are indeed helpful and kind, but are they truly selfless? Perhaps not[17] — people help others for a "paid back[18]" in some way.

⑭ 不需要这么复杂的逻辑转来转去，删去。同时 although 后面不能接动词，非要接可以接个 futile in his efforts。

⑮ to help himself extricate from 改为 extricate himself from；extricate 后面要接反身代词。

⑯ 表达啰嗦，改为 Are their deeds beneficial?

⑰ Perhaps not 与全文第一句那么斩钉截铁的"大家都自私"语气不对应，与全文一边倒的观点不符合。可改为：Of course not。

⑱ 改为 reward 更合适。

【文章分析】

大家可能也看出来了，与第六篇文章类似，本文也属于观点奇特的一类。与第七篇比，文字功底差些，但分数却高些，胜在论证得力，脉络分明。

因为他的观点是"利他主义的本质是利己"，虽然不中听，却旗帜鲜明，一竿子到底。

中国几千年前就有"性善论"与"性恶论"之争，人的本性向来是作家们要揭示的永恒主题。

Frankenstein 这个怪物的行为有目的性，作者就认定他的利他行为具有利己的目的，这可以说得过去。而且这个事例也表明作者阅读面比较广泛。一般而言，SAT 考官对于这样举自己读过的书为例子会有所偏爱。

第二个例子，举加拿大在世界大战时参战，为战后赢得独立主权创造了有利条件，更是锦上添花，为文章增加了不少说服力。

论证从个体到国家,从童话到现实,层次非常鲜明。

这是 2008 年 10 月的真题作文,作者是笔者的一名学生,在笔者刚刚修改完她的这篇文章后不到一个小时,就接到她的电话,得知她被加州大学伯克利分校和纽约大学 Stern 商学院同时录取的喜讯。

第九篇　成功和快乐取决于什么

（7分真题作文）

Think carefully about the issue presented in the following excerpt and the assignment below：

> Everybody has some choice. People are always blaming their circumstances for what they are. I don't believe in circumstances. The people who get on in this world are the people who get up and look for the circumstances they want and, if they can't find them, make them.

Assignment：Do success and happiness depend on the choices people make rather than on factors beyond their control? Plan and write an essay in which you develop your point of view on this issue. Support your position with reasoning and examples taken from your reading, studies, experience, or observations.

【学生原作】

Success and happiness largely depend on the choices people make, but occasionally they also depend on factors beyond our① control. Success comes with hard work and opportunity②. If people are not prepared, they will not be able to seize the opportunities open to them③.

① 应该是 their 和句子中的 people 匹配。

② Success comes with hard work and opportunity.（原文）

Both hard work and opportunity are essential on the road to success.（改进版）

这两句话着重点不同。第一句强调的是 success；第二句强调 hard work 与 opportunity，符合本文的意图。

③ open to them 过于呆板，为增加文章活泼度，可改为 even when the lady of fortune knocks on the door。

_____④My family moved to Canada in 2000. _____⑤ and my father had been to many job fairs and none of them was successful because he did not have local trainings⑥ at the time. To make matter worse⑦, the economy of British Columbia was in a recession, which pretty much diminished his chance of obtaining a job. My mother advised him to enroll in the local university and he agreed⑧. After two years of study, he graduated with a degree in Mining Engineering. At the graduation ceremony, he, by chance, ran into an executive of Major Corporation⑨ whose son is also part of the graduating class⑩ and they chatted for a while.

④ 此处加 Take my father as an example,作为过渡！

⑤ It was a brand new beginning for me, but a difficult choice for my father, a middle aged man with a family to support. 可以加入上面这句话,刻画出一个沧桑的移民父亲形象,开始煽情。一般而言,例子段落开头放缓节奏,让读者喘口气,期待一下,可以让作者厚积薄发。

⑥ He frequented job fairs 比 my father had been to many job fairs 更生动。

and 不能体现转折关系,应改为 but。

把 none of them... 改为 he found no luck because he lacked the so-called local training,加一个"so-called"可传达作者的态度,继续煽情！

⑦ 改成 To make things worse。

⑧ agreed 不如用 followed her advice 更具体清晰。

⑨ 非特指,应小写,加不定冠词。

⑩ "儿子是班级的一部分",汉语是对的,英文中这样就不对等了。应改成 son is also a member of the graduating class。

The next morning, _____⑪ my dad received a phone call from that executive he met earlier and that executive⑫ asked my dad to join the mining division of his company. In fact, they needed to find⑬ a team of experienced engineering to work with Rio Tinto because Rio had forecasted a strong demand of⑭ commodities from developing countries.

⑪ 在此加入 there came a miracle! 煽情达到顶峰,兼有故事发展的里程碑功能。

⑫ 使用"who"从句,更紧凑。

⑬ form a team 更合适。

⑭ 应该是 demand for something,属于介词误用。

Now looking back to this event, the conclusion I can come up with is⑮ success comes when preparation meets opportunity，even if the opportunity happens purely by chance and luck. _____⑯（**242 words**）

⑮ 主语 conclusion 和状语 looking 变成了悬垂错误，应该是 I come up with the conclusion that ...

⑯ 文章中的感想少了点。可以加上 It seems that hard work is the avenue while opportunity is the street. The moment they meet each other, a crossroad is formed, making success inevitable 这样的话。本句使用 avenue 与 street 交叉的概念，表达出在努力与机会同时具备的情况下，个人成功的必然性。比喻生动，大家可以参考。

【文章分析】

文章有两个大的毛病，其一，整个文章是一个自然段，铁板一块（这里为了分析方便，把原文切成四段），读者无法体会到故事的发展、思维的深入；其二，文章举了一个非常贴切的例子，却因为过于平淡的叙述，好故事被讲得毫无趣味性，非常可惜！

针对这两个大的毛病，我们把原文分了段，加了有趣的句子，活泼了文风。

要注意，讲故事也要分段，段落之间要有衔接句子，这是我们想拿 SAT 高分必须要学会的结构常识。其次，要夹叙夹议，添油加醋，把一盘材料好的菜做出风味来。

第十篇　我们应该崇拜英雄而不是名人
（文章一，8分真题作文）

Think carefully about the issue presented in the following excerpt and the assignment below：

> Having many admirers is one way to become a celebrity，but it is not the way to become a hero. Heroes are self-made. Yet in our daily lives we see no difference between "celebrities" and "heroes." For this reason, we deprive ourselves of real role models. We should admire heroes — people who are famous because they are great — but not celebrities — people who simply seem great because they are famous.
>
> Adapted from Daniel Boorstin, *The Image：A Guide to Pseudo-Events in America*

Assignment：Should we admire heroes but not celebrities? Plan and write an essay in which you develop your point of view on this issue. Support your position with reasoning and examples taken from your reading，studies，experience，or observations.

【学生原作】

In this day and age①，heroes and celebrities are somehow blended together②. We have a difficult time determining who is a celebrity and who is a hero because the media usually glorifies some celebrities as heroes and vice versa. In reality, however，heroes are ordinary people accomplishing extraordinary feats and they are the true heroes③ people should admire.

① In this day 就够了，或者直接说 Nowadays。

② blend together 改为 exchangeable terms。

③ true hero 这个概念本身没有错，但用在此文中就不妥当了。本来就在分析 hero 与 celebrity 的区别，你再把 hero 分成 true hero 与 untrue hero，这不添乱嘛！

Real heroes④ usually conceal themselves; not the kind of secret identity people would think of, but they do it⑤ because they want to help people anonymously and stay out of glorification. For example, your parents could be the greatest heroes in your life but you don't easily recognize what they do is so great⑥. Sometimes we just take these things for granted; we⑦ never learn to appreciate the "insignificant" chores they do. For instance, the breakfast on ⑧ you eat before going to⑨ school is prepared by somebody⑩. The meal won't cook itself; it takes efforts, time and energy. ⑪

④ 道理同③,尽量避免出现新概念。

⑤ it 指代不明。

⑥ recognize 后面直接加名词 greatness,文风更简洁。

⑦ 注意把 we 改成 you,文章忌讳"we""you"夹杂,应保持阐述角度的统一。

⑧ 明显的笔误,删除。

⑨ 悬垂错误,breakfast 能发出 going to school 的动作吗?

⑩ somebody 指代不明,此处明明在歌颂父母,为什么不用 your parents 呢?

⑪ 这句话直接删去,放在这里显得啰嗦。

Some celebrities just simply don't deserve that much of our admiration because they have not worked for their fame or accomplished anything. In fact, many pop stars have gone out of their way to make themselves the headline of gossip magazines. They may resort to streaking, making a big scene out of nothing, or even deliberately exposing private body parts to paparazzi. Some kids idolize those celebrities' fame and fortune and think those are their⑫ role models, which they clearly are not. _____⑬

⑫ 连续出现 those 与 their 两个词,可改为 take them as。

⑬ 可以举个名人的小例子,如 Lindsey Lohan 等,以求生动具体。Take Lindsay Lohan as an example. She achieved fame at a very early age by taking the lead role in "The Parent Trap" and "Mean Girls", and thus she was once the hottest young actress standing for the young generation born in the 80s. Yet her drug-abuse together with other negative news almost ruined her life, and these all made her no longer suitable to be hold as an idol of younger generation's admiration. She could be regarded as celebrity, but there is no way that she is a hero.

Like what the prompt says, celebrities are people who seem great because they are famous. When you take that magnifying glass and examine bits and parts of what they do, you will find little, if nothing, to learn from them except from their mistakes. _____ ⑭ (*279 words*)

⑭ 文章结尾段,想象丰富,但批判有余,客观不足。SAT 作文中,不能把事情讲得太死,否则考官会认为你看事物过于片面,这也是本文语言好但分并不高的另一个原因。可以把本段语气放缓和点,改为:Like what the prompt says, celebrities are people who seem great only because they are famous. Makeup can make an ordinary girl look like a superstar in a second, but cannot turn her into a heroine; in the same way, fame and money can decorate people, but can not transform them from inside. We need the guidance of inspiring deeds of heroes to lead us in the process of life and to tell truth from lie.

【文章分析】

文章开头指出中心观点,人们应该崇拜的是英雄,而非名人。

第二段,英雄是什么? 是普通人,完成了非常的事情。特别指出,父母也是英雄。

第三段,从反面论证有很多名人其实道德败坏,不应该被人崇拜。

结尾段,再次对名人的价值进行怀疑。

本文结构清晰,过渡合理,属于比较难得的好结构。

本文语言功底比较扎实,文风比较符合西方人的审美,但为什么分数依然不高呢? 欠缺在内容缺少 concrete example(有说服力的例子),也就是"有骨头没肉"。我们东方人比较喜欢抽象,写文章也只需论理即可。但 SAT 作文最喜欢"指名道姓",何况是这么样好写的与 heroes, celebrities 有关的题目! 大家耳熟能详的 Michale Jackson, Britney Spears, Brad Pitt, Lindsey Lohan 等等,哪个没有反面新闻呢?

第十一篇　我们应该崇拜英雄而不是名人
（文章二，10 分真题作文）

Think carefully about the issue presented in the following excerpt and the assignment below：

> Having many admirers is one way to become a celebrity, but it is not the way to become a hero. Heroes are self-made. Yet in our daily lives we see no difference between "celebrities" and "heroes." For this reason, we deprive ourselves of real role models. We should admire heroes — people who are famous because they are great — but not celebrities — people who simply seem great because they are famous.
>
> Adapted from Daniel Boorstin, *The Image: A Guide to Pseudo-Events in America*

Assignment：Should we admire heroes but not celebrities? Plan and write an essay in which you develop your point of view on this issue. Support your position with reasoning and examples taken from your reading, studies, experience, or observations.

学生原作：

In our daily life, we should both admire these heroes and celebrities because <u>some celebrities are just those heroes</u>①. We should honor their merit and dignity and <u>should be learned by all of us</u>②, <u>for example, just like</u>③ Djingo, a famous guitar player.

① Prompt 中对于 hero celebrities 给了截然不同的定义：heroes — people who are famous because they are great；celebrities — people who simply seem great because they are famous。考生可以二选一，或者是倾向其中一方。这位学生开头一句话就玩了个文字游戏，把英雄和名人的界限去掉（some celebrities are just those heroes）。这条道路好走，虽然有点冒风险。

② 并列句中，如果主语已经不同，那么就不能省略主语。这里要改为 they

should be learned by all of us。

③ for example，just like 都是举例，功能重复了，去掉 for example。另外，for example 后面必须要接句子，如果是接个名词结构，要写成 such as。

Some celebrities are well known because they are ＿＿＿＿④ heroes，like Djingo，a distinguished guitar player，through his accomplishments to show his value and meaning of life⑤. Djingo began to play guitar at tender age of 13，and he gained skills so quickly that at the age of 18，he was regarded as a professional. But he was merely a professional⑥ until he was twenty when an event occurred that forever changed his style and sealed his fate.⑦

④ 既然作者已经在第一段把 hero 与 celebrity 划等号，这里可以再加一个 also。

⑤ 这里需要一个定语从句 who showed his value and meaning of life through his accomplishments。

⑥ merely a professional：professional 与 merely 搭配有贬低专业人士之意，且这不太符合我们的常识（"他仅仅是个专家"，专家还不够吗？）。可以换为中性语气的 no more than a professional。

⑦ 这个词组用得很地道。

One day，he went home with a birthday cake，the wick that fell out of candle accidentally ignited the highly flammable plastic furrowers stored at home.⑧ The house turned into an inferno in just a few seconds. Fortunately⑨ Djingo escaped conflagratio⑩，but with heavy loss — one leg was amputated and his left hand is severely crippled that only two of the five fingers remain in function. It seemed that Djingo's life would come to a stop here. But it is this event that distinguished him from the common guitar players⑪. Djingo didn't give up. After recovery，he soon involved in⑫ his music career，practicing systematically and working persistently on a new method that can get around with his loss of three fingers. Finally，he devised a chord progression that was peerless in the realm of jazz music. Then⑬ he was treated as a jazz pioneer. Djingo is a celebrity but also a hero⑭.

⑧ 这是串句现象，需要把 cake 后的逗号改为句号，在本句前加上 Unexpectedly，以表达意想不到的事情要发生。

⑨ Fortunately 后面要有逗号。

⑩ conflagration 前要有定冠词 the。

⑪ 应该在 distinguished 前面加上 finally,句子会更通顺点,也和作者的意图相吻合。

⑫ involve 一般用被动结构最多(也可用主动结构),结构为: be involved in sth /doing sth。这里可改为:He was involved in ...

⑬ Then 一般表达小转折。这里整个故事已经讲完(前面已经出现了 finally),我们需要一个总结性的大词,改用 After this 或 As a result。

⑭ 不平行,Not only ... but also 要成对出现。另外作为段尾句,应该要在思想上提高点,句子也要长点,才压得住。可改为:From this, we can see that Djingo is not only a celebrity but also a hero。

Djingo is _____⑮ the only person with disability that interferes with his profession: Beethoven was deaf, Picasso with madness.⑯ They all overcome adversities and become heroes. They are the people we should honour. (***305 words***)

⑮ sb. is not the only person ...(某人不是惟一的……),这里明显少了个 not

⑯ 毕加索 Pablo Picasso (1881—1973)是西班牙画家、雕塑家,是现代艺术(立体派)的创始人,西方现代派绘画的主要代表。他没有发疯过,作者可能把他与可怜的荷兰画家梵高 Vincent Van Gogh (1853~1890)弄混了。除此之外,句子还有不平行的缺点。可改为:Beethoven became deaf but still composed Symphony No. 9, Van Goah alternated between fits of madness and lucidity but painted the world-known *Sunflower*。

【文章分析】

这是笔者一名学生的投机取巧之作,据说该生言必称 Djingo,"Djingo means Bingo"成为此生所创名言。笔者对他无比佩服,因他告诉我,凡是 SAT 的作文题,有很多题目都能把 Djingo 拿来说事,只需开头结尾稍微改换下门面。他这样写文章总是拿一个非常典型的事例来说话,从另外一个角度说明,平时总结五到六个典型例子(不是像爱迪生那样"地球人都知道"的例子)对我们写文章是大有裨益的。

总之,记好了,Djingo means Bingo!

第十二篇　归属于一个团体是否有价值
（6分真题作文）

Think carefully about the issue presented in the following excerpt and the assignment below.

> Since we live in a global society, surely we should view ourselves as citizens of the whole world. But instead, people choose to identify and associate with smaller and more familiar groups. People think of themselves as belonging to families, nations, cultures, and generations — or as belonging to smaller groups whose members share ideas, views, or common experiences. All of these kinds of groups may offer people a feeling of security but also prevent them from learning or experiencing anything new.

Assignment：Is there any value for people to belong only to a group or groups with which they have something in common? Plan and write an essay in which you develop your point of view on this issue. Support your position with reasoning and examples taken from your reading, studies, experience, or observations.

【学生原作】

In the world we live in today, there are so many different cultures coexist① in one region due to massive immigration, which made rapid growth possible②. Some cultures often hold conflicting value③ with other cultures. Therefore, people gets together with somebody they can relate to is a natural phenomenon④.

① 应该是 coexisting。

② 和上下文没有什么联系，删去。

③ 应该是 values。

④ 此处为主语从句，应该在 people 前加上 that，不然动词 is 没有主语与之匹配。

One reason people form group is because⑤ they fear that people from other cultures won't accept them or devalue⑥ their traditions or simply people do not understand each other. Throughout the continent⑦, people form groups based on ethnicity or religion. For example, Jewish National congress, Chinese student association,⑧ African American Environmentalist Association etc. On a global scale, al-Qaida, a terrorist organization, recruits young men to kill people. This brings us to the question of exploiting religion for political interests. Clearly, none of the Middle Eastern countries can officially declare war on NATO's member states. So al-Qaida was created by its leader Osama bin Laden and his allies to declare Jihad on the West, which targets civilians instead of the military. Since bin Laden cannot do everything himself, he must recruit radical young men to carry out his ambitions. By joining a group, people gain strength to take on formidable rivals.

⑤ 这里的 because 一定要改为 that。中文说"原因是什么"，在英文里，应该是 that 从句。

⑥ devalue（使）贬值，用 belittle、look down upon 或 discount 更好。

⑦ Throughout the continent 中的 continent 来得无厘头，应该是 Throughout the world。

⑧ 组织机构，首字母最好大写，而且要统一。另外，For example 后面不是句子，应该用 Such as，同时把 For example 前的句号改为逗号。

It seems that to people who join a group, it is the only way to gain whether it is economical, political or personal ambitions⑨. Together they can accomplish a lot more than individuals. The groups are more powerful in influencing the decisions made by governments around the world⑩, sometimes they resort to despicable violence⑪ for their own gain.（*257 words*）

⑨ 句子结构七零八落。作为结尾段，应该铿锵有力，不要出现 It seems that 这样犹豫的表达。改为 People join a group to gain economical and political benefits and to achieve personal ambitions。

⑩ 还是句子结构问题。作为状语，around the world 最好单独放在句首。the decisions made by governments 太啰嗦，可直接用 government decisions。全句改为 Around the world, the groups are more powerful in influencing the government decisions。另外，最后一句的意思比较模糊，同时出现了串句错误，应该在 sometimes 前加上连词。

⑪ despicable violence 为"可鄙的暴力"。终于在文章结尾出现了一个贬低恐怖组织的词语,但已经太晚了。整个句子可翻译为:"在影响政府决策方面,团体更有力量;有时候(团体)会使用可鄙的暴力维护自己的利益"。最后这个分句使作者的观点重新陷入一片模糊中。到底是团体还是不支持?到文章最后一句话都没有讲明白。

【文章分析】

全文败在所举的例子上。作者或许是语言功底不够深厚,句里行间对恐怖分子本·拉登及基地组织毫无贬低之意,甚至有向往之倾向。可以说,这个例子导致两个考官同时都只给 6 分中的 3 分。美国人最忌讳的人和事,被考生拿来做正面的例子,而且还说他们"团结起来力量大"(By joining a group, people gain strength to take on formidable rivals),效果可以想象是如何的"震撼",直接震到 3 分了。可见,SAT 作文中,举例最好不要举这种政治性太强的。

大家千万注意少碰这些雷区,除了以恐怖组织为代表的政治题材,类似的还有堕胎、同性恋等等道德题材;这些观点美国人自己还在争,你的观点不一定讨考官喜欢。就算他们在观点方面非常宽容,我们也不要太指望他们给出高分。

第四章　SAT 作文漫谈：遣词造句和句式结构

第一节　语言的简洁性

简练的文字是一种美德，英文中有一句话说的就是这个意思：Brevity is a virtue. 为什么说是一种美德呢，因为你节约了读者的时间和精力。

在英文写作中，要做到能用一个词表达的意思，绝不要用两个词，能用一句话表达清楚的意思，就绝不要用两个句子。许多学生的作文里，充斥着毫无必要的修饰性单词，一方面浪费了读者的时间，另外一方面也使文章和句子的核心意思受到影响。

表达累赘的一个重要原因是学生在写作的思考过程中，多多少少受到中文的影响。中文的一个特点是"虚"词很多，很多学生在把中文转化到英文的时候，往往会都把那些"虚"词带到英文中去，结果写出很多中式英文。

例：使用这个方法能解决你目前的问题。

直译：~~The use of~~ This method will solve your current problem.

其实，在这个英文句子里，我们要把 The use of 删除，变成 This method will solve your current problem，不仅保留了原文意思，又非常简洁。问题是为什么同学们在写作时候会把这个 use 加上呢？说到底，还是受到了中文"使用"这个词的影响。在英文表达里，把 The use of 加上，反而冲淡了 method 的核心作用。

例：我们要加强国防现代化建设的步伐。

直译：We must speed up ~~the pace of~~ the construction of the national defense.

这种表达非常累赘，同时把核心动词和动作对象分割太远。如果把划线部分删除，变成：We must speed up the national defense，不仅表达清晰，也避免了一些累赘词。简化后的句子，更加有力量。Speed up 本身就有加快步伐的含义，pace 放在那是多余的。

下面的例句都存在累赘之处，不符合英文表达习惯。

1. The search of the forest that they ~~conducted~~ was ~~entirely~~ complete.

   →They conducted a complete search of the forest.

   →Or：Their search of the forest is complete.

   （complete 本身就有 entirely 的意思，所以 entirely 的修饰没有必要。conducted 用在此处是多余的，写上 conducted 是因为受到了中文"进行"的影响。）

2. It ~~makes me feel~~ painful to think that she has to work 12 hours a day.

   →It pains me to think that she has to work 12 hours a day.

   （中文喜欢说"什么使我怎么样"，很多同学用英文表达此义时喜欢用 it makes me feel 加形容词的结构。而英语可直接用一个动词把这个意思表达出来。）

3. When you come to the second traffic light，turn right.

   →Turn right at the second traffic light.

   （中文喜欢先说从句，而英文喜欢把主句的意思先说出来，让读者知道这个句子要说什么，然后再用从句补充必要的意思。本句改动后，把一个复杂句改成了简单句，巧妙使用了介词结构。）

4. The next step to take is to finish the difficult job in a quick way.

   →The next step is to finish the job in a quick way.

   （中文说"下面要采取一个步骤"，所以许多同学转化到英文里就是 the next step to take，而这个 to take 纯属多余，和 the use of this method 中的 the use of 如出一辙。）

5. I sat there speechless, nodding my head to show my approval.

   →I sat there speechless, nodding my agreement.

   （nod 本身的意思就是点头，所以 my head 是多余的。nodding my agreement 是非常地道的英文表达。）

在英文里，我们在表达否定概念时，习惯于加 not，其实很多时候可以使用一个特定的字来表达同样的概念，从而使语言简洁。比如，尽量使用 disagree，而不是 not agree，用 sad 要比用 not happy 简练些。

例：学生没有经济支持，是很难读完大学的。

A student may find it difficult to finish his college if he doesn't have financial backing.

如果把 doesn't have 写成 lack，不仅仅表达同样的意思，也使文字更加简练了。

同样，unauthorized money 要好于 money that is not authorized；persevere 要好过 not give up。

在英文，这样的例子比比皆是，平时要多注意收集整理。

例：我住在温哥华是因为它的交通很方便。

I choose to stay in Vancouver because its communication is convenient.

改进后的句子：I choose to stay in Vancouver due to its convenient communication. 改进后的句子表达同样的意思，但是避免使用一个复杂句，从而使文字精炼很多。

在英文里，有些词本身已经含有某种特定的意思，在使用这类词时，要尽量避免再用一些不必要的修饰词，以免句意重复。

比如，"人民的生活水平"，直接说 living standard 就可以了，因为 living standard 只能是指人，但总是见到学生写成 people's living standard；"农业大丰收"，说 harvest 就可以了，但就是一些正规的出版物上也能看到"agricultural harvest"这样的表达。harvest 本来就是指农业的，前面加上 agricultural 就是句意重复了。

例：学校当局正采取一系列措施来解决当前的问题。

The school authorities are taking a series of measures to solve the current problems.

a series of 纯属多余，因为 measures 已经包含了复数的概念。

第二节 动词的使用

动词是句子的核心,动词使用贴切、到位,会使整个句子非常活泼,起到画龙点睛的作用。相反,动词使用不当或死板,就会使整个句子缺少生气,枯燥乏味。

动词使用的一个重要原则是要恰当,要深刻了解一个动词的内在含义,不能望文生义,想当然地随便使用一个动词。

例:一道闪电出现在天空。

A bolt of lighting ~~appeared~~ *flashed* in the sky.

在这里,appeared 显然是使用不当,说一个东西 appear 在一个地方,起码这个东西会 stay for a while,而闪电是转瞬即逝的。原句给人的感觉是闪电似乎在天空上一直闪现(那不是闪电,是彩虹)。所以,这个 appeared 应该写成 flashed,以把握闪电转瞬即逝的感觉。

动词使用恰当,还可以避免一些不必要的修饰词,从而使句子更加简练,同时又可以达到生动自然的效果。

例:老师快速地读了我的句子并改正了一些拗口的表达。

My teacher ~~read~~ *scanned* my sentence ~~quickly corrected~~ *ironed out* my awkward expressions.

该句中的 read my sentence quickly 如果表达为 scan my sentence 就很简练,因为 scan 本身就包括了速度;另外,correct 的使用也不是很贴切,因为 awkward expression 不算是错误,所以用 correct 就不如用 iron out(使更加贴切通顺)更地道。

例:Mary ~~walked~~ *stormed* into the store ~~angrily~~ and ~~asked~~ *demanded* for a refund.

首先,ask for 的使用不是很地道,因为既然"怒气冲冲",就不会有这么委婉的 ask for 了,故改为 demand 以和前文的 angrily 相吻合。同样,walked into the store angrily,完全可以用一个词 storm 表示,因为 storm 用作动词时,就有怒气冲冲的意思。全句改为 Mary stormed into the store and demanded a refund.

在平时的英文学习中,一定要多注意积累动词,并且要对一个动词所表达的深刻内涵有把握。动词掌握得越多,在表达自己思想的时候会越有主动性。如说到"提高"或"上升",不能光用 increase,还有好多更地道的表达呢,如 jump, surge, soar, skyrocket 等等。如表示"下降",不要总围绕"decrease"打转转,为什么不根据需要有选择地使用像 shrink, drop, shed, sink, plummet 等等这样有特定含义的词呢?

下面几个例句中的动词使用都不是很恰当，或者不是很地道，而修改后的句子动词都变得地道贴切了。

1. He drove the car around the corner in a cautious way.

   →He negotiated around the corner.

   （negotiate 本身有小心绕过、经过的意思。）

2. "Bravo"，the audience uttered the words almost at the same time.

   → "Bravo"，the audience choired.

   （既然是同时讲一个词，那干脆就用 choir 好了。choir 的意思是"合唱，"既然是合唱，那就要异口同声。）

3. The fabulous academic performance by the new student made all other students in the class less important.

   →The fabulous academic performance by the new student dwarfed all other students in the class.

   （使别人黯然失色，就是 dwarf，这个词的本意是"侏儒"，当作动词使用就是使 something 或 somebody 相形见绌或黯然失色。）

4. My mom thought that the cost for the trip would be around ＄2 000.

   →My mom calculated that the cost for the trip would be around ＄2 000.

   （我们中文只要说到"认为"，大家几乎都会想到用 think，但是还有别的字可用，比如这里的"认为"涉及数字和金额，所以用 calculate 就比较恰当。当我们要表达经过认真思考后的"认为"，用 decide 就比较合适。比如：After talking with many friends，I finally decided that Mary should be my life partner。）

5. Mary plays computer games every day.

   →Mary is steeped into the computer games every day.

   （说 Mary 每天打游戏，用 be steeped in 这个词组就很好，这个词组的意思是"沉浸于"，用在这里非常合适。）

在现代英文中，一个非常流行的趋势就是大量的名词、形容词，甚至副词被当作动词来使用。从名词转化过来的动词，可以定义为具体动词，这类动词很容易让人产生联想，因而受到现代英文的青睐。

例：小路弯弯曲曲通向森林。

一般的说法是：The road winds its way into the forest. 这样的说法当然没有问题，但是，wind 这个字属于抽象动词，不能让读者产生什么相关的联想，如果把这个句子写成 The road snakes down into the forest 就大不一样了。snake 用作名词是"蛇"的意思，在这里，被用作了动词，很容易让读者产生联想，把小路蜿蜒曲折的样子给生动地描写出来了。

在现代英文中，这样的例子比比皆是。

我们看美国 TIME 杂志上一篇关于伊拉克报道里的一句话。Quasay was secretive, politically ruthless, hardworking and so idolatrous of his father that he <u>aped</u> his clothing style, bushy mustache and choice of cigar.

这里的 ape 用做名词的意思是类人猿，在这里被活用为动词，意思是"模仿"。为什么呢？ape 的一个特点就是喜欢模仿人类动作，把一个事物的特点用作动词，可以说是非常巧妙。显然，这里用 ape 要比使用 imitate 这样的抽象动词更生动活泼。

不是什么名词都可以转化成动词的，可转化的大概可以归为以下几个类别：

动物

We shall not be <u>foxed</u> (duped) by his tricks.

He was so hungry that he <u>wolfed</u> (devour) down 3 bowls of rice within one minute.

身体的一部分

I <u>eyed</u> him with suspicion. （注意，eye 后面不可再加介词 at 了。）

Don't <u>nose</u> around. （不要四处打探。）

A man should <u>shoulder</u> the family responsibilities.

I will <u>back</u> you up. （我会支持你的。）

一些表职位的词

He has been <u>bossing</u> that company for 10 years.

The woman put all her mind into <u>nursing</u> the child.

一些抽象名词

What he said did <u>anger</u> his girlfriend.

I have been <u>hungering</u> for a formal education in Western countries.

当然，现代英文里也有很多形容词和副词转化为动词的例子。比如 slow down, better people's life, empty（倾倒）the chemicals into the river 等等。同学们在学习过程中要善于发现和总结，看见一个记一个，并在自己的作文练习中学会使用它们。

第三节　避免使用悬垂结构

在英文写作中,许多学生常犯的一个错误就是大量使用悬垂结构。

现在分词(V-ing)或过去分词(V-ed)在句子中作状语时,其逻辑主语(即该动作的发出者)从文法的要求来看,必须是句子的主语;但如果该主语和现在分词或过去分词在逻辑上没有联系,那么现在分词或过去分词就变成了一个没有依附的分词了,文法上称这样的错误为悬垂修饰。

例: After reading the book, _____.

a. I fed the dog

b. the dog was fed by me

c. feeding the dog was his task

d. the dog was hungry

因为 reading the book 为状语,作为主语的成分就必须是 reading the book 的动作发出者。在各选项中,只有 a 的主语符合条件,而其他选项的主语均不能作为 reading the book 的动作发出者,故正确选项为 a。

写作时,当句子以 V-ing 或 V-ed 开头时(有时在 V-ing 或 V-ed 前有 after、before、while 或 when 之类的连词),首先要考虑到句子的主语必须和该 V-ing 或 V-ed 在逻辑上有关系,否则就犯了悬垂结构的错误。

详细说来,当句子以 V-ing 开头,则主句必须是该动作发出者;当句子以 V-ed 开头,则主句必须和该 V-ed 构成被动关系。

例: a. Writing in a free style, the novelist is popular among the children.

b. Written in a free style, the novel is popular among the children.

在 a 句中,write 动作是由主语 the novelist 发出的,故采用 V-ing 形式。

在 b 句中,the novel 是被写的,故采用 V-ed 形式。

为使大家对悬垂结构有进一步了解,我们来分析下列例句:

a. Waiting for a bus, a brick fell on my head.

b. Driving on the road that night, a squirrel suddenly leapt out of the jungle.

c. Getting down from the bus, my ankle was sprained.

d. Looking out of the window, there were many people on the streets.

e. Sitting under an apple tree one night, a new idea came to Newton.

f. Looking in this way, the situation didn't seem that bad.

g. <u>Writing</u> in a free style，<u>the novelist</u> is popular.

h. <u>Ranked</u> as one of the top ten university，<u>many students</u> are eager to have the chance to study in Princeton.

【分析】

a. 错。因为 brick 不能发出 writing 这样的动作,应改为:

Waiting for a bus,I was hit by a brick.

b. 错。因为 a squirrel 不能发出 driving 这样的动作。既然主语必须是能发出 driving 动作的成分,应改为:

Driving on the road that night,Tom saw a squirrel leaping out of the jungle.

c. 错。My ankle 不能发出 getting down 的动作。

d. 错。There 也不能发出 look out of 的动作。

e. 错。是 Newton 发出 sit 的动作,所以句子的主语必须是 Newton,可以改为

Sitting under an apple tree on night，Newton came up with a new idea。

f. 错。Situation 应该是被 looked 的,所以,looking 要改为 looked。

g. 正确,novelist 发出 write 的动作。

h. 错。是 Princeton 被 ranked as one of the top ten universities,所以句子的主语必须是 Princeton,可以改为 Ranked as one of the top ten universities, Princeton is the choice by many students who are eager to have the chance to learn there。

第四节 学会使用同位结构

同位结构(Appositive Structure)是指句子中指代同一事物的两个名词或词组构成一个同位关系,简单说,就是一个较长的名词或是词组对相邻的一个名词进行进一步的解释说明。同位结构一般要求一先一后,位置相邻。使用同位结构可以大大简化句子结构,使句子的核心词更加突出,从而起到强调的作用。

例:Mary, a pretty girl, is popular among the boys.

在上句中,a pretty girl 为名词性结构,对名词 Mary 进行补充说明。这样,Mary 和 a pretty girl 就构成一组同位结构。

使用同位结构能使句子更加简洁清晰。在上述句子中,如果不使用同位结构,则该句必须写成:

Mary is a pretty girl and she is popular among the boys.

这样,原句本来是一个简单句,由于没有使用同位结构,而变成了复合句。

例:His only interest in life is reading novels and it has brought him much enjoyment.

上面的复合句,如使用同位结构,可简化成:

His only interest in life, reading novels, has brought him much enjoyment.

这样,only interest in life 和 reading novels 构成了一组同位结构,把原句由复合句简化为简单句。

再看以下几个同位结构的实例:

Have you ever read the life of George Washington, the first President of the U. S. A?

The Yangtze River, the longest river in China, runs through 17 provinces.

Thomas, my best friend in Vancouver, paid a visit to me yesterday.

Acoustics, the science of sound, is an abstract subject.

使用同位结构不仅仅可以简化句子,而且可以使句子更加完美和平行。我们可以通过下面两句话的比较更深刻地体会一下使用同位结构的美妙之处。

原句:George Bernard Shaw, whose father was shiftless and alcoholic and whose mother was strong-minded and musically gifted，was born in Dublin in 1856.

使用同位结构后可以写成：

George Bernard Shaw was born in Dublin in 1856，the son of a shiftless and alcoholic father and a strong-minded and musically gifted mother.

改正后的句子首先把主语和主要动词就近摆放，使句子核心意思立刻呈现出来，再通过一个同位结构为核心句子进一步补充必要的细节，句子结构层次清楚，重点突出，同时也做到了平行完美。

随着科技的进步，大量的新词语不断地被吸收到英文中来。在英文写作中，有时候要对这些新词语进行适当的解释，因而同位结构的使用越来越频繁。

刚才我们谈到的同位结构是比较简单的一种，英文中比较复杂的一种同位结构，常常会出现在 SAT 语法试题里。

例：Ancient Chinese people believed that rice has therapeutic function，a belief that has been dominant in Chinese culture.

这个例子可看作是一种特殊同位结构的运用。在一个完整句子的逗号后面，用一个抽象名词来概括逗号前面句子的内容，然后再用一个分句或结构对该抽象名词进行进一步修饰或说明。这样，这个抽象名词和其前面的整个句子（有时是句子的某一重要组成部分）构成一种同位关系。

使用这样的同位结构往往是为了起到强调的效果，同时也是对前文所叙述的内容进行进一步的补充。

例：I failed my exam and lost my girlfriend，a situation that I had never encountered in the before.

在上句中，用 a situation 对 I failed my exam and lost my girlfriend 进行总结概述，在 situation 后用一个从句对它进行进一步修饰，从而使 situation 和前面的完整句子构成一种特殊的同位结构。

在这种特殊的同位结构中，有时不是用一个特殊抽象名词（如上述句子中的 a belief，a situation）对前面句子的内容进行总结概述，而只是对前面的某一名词进行简单重复。这种重复是一种修辞手段，以达到强调的效果。

例：We are living in a most dangerous age，an age marked by biological warfare and atomic bombs.

上句中，对 age 进行重复是一种修辞手段，是用 an age 后的分词结构来对 a

dangerous age 进行进一步修饰，以达到生动的效果。

例：George Washington was a legend <u>in his time</u>, <u>a time</u> which is awakened by domestic strives, escalating warfare and a profusion of warring factions.

由同位结构进一步简化，演化成一种可以称为"独立形容词"的结构，即用一个或数个形容词对某一邻近的名词进行进一步修饰。

例：Mary, a pretty girl, is popular with the boys. （同位结构）
Pretty, Mary is popular with the boys. （独立形容词结构）
使用独立形容词结构要比使用同位结构更能简化句子。

例：The trees are strong and tall and they have survived another severe winter.
若使用独立形容词结构，可写为：
Strong and tall, the trees have survived another severe winter.

例：Mary was angry, and she threw away the flowers.
若使用独立形容词结构，可写为：
Angry, Mary threw away the flowers.
这个句子中，把 angry 这个表达核心意义的词单独拿出来，既简洁，又使与 angry 有密切关系的 Mary 与其紧密相邻，从而使句意表达更加有效。

第五节 学会使用现在分词结构

现在分词结构是动词原形加-ing形式,这是同学们都比较熟悉的一种结构,但对其用法和奥妙却知之甚少。使用现在分词结构可以大大简化句子,同时,由于分词自身的一些特点,可以起到意想不到的效果。

例:Mary dislikes English and it makes her mom angry.

这个句子看上去很简单,意思似乎也是清楚的,但仔细研究会发现这个貌似简单正确的句子存在下面一些问题。

首先,谈 it 的指代问题。从句意上看,it 只能指代 Mary dislikes English 这样的一件事情,但 it 指代整个句子的内容,本身是一些语法专家所不能接受的。

另外,这个句子是个复合句,and 前面表达一个原因,and 后面的句子表达一个结果,就是说整个句子是个因果关系,而表达因果关系的句子用 and 来连接就稍显不妥了。

最后,英文习惯用一个完整的句子来表达重要的内容,而次要的内容要用从句或短语来表达,这样就会使整个句子重点突出。就本句而言,Mary 不喜欢英文是全句的核心内容,应该用主句形式表达,而 Mary 不喜欢英文导致的结果多种多样,让她妈妈生气只是结果的一种,显然应该用从句或短语的形式来表达比较妥当。and 把前后内容的重要性并列了,就是说,and 前后的句子从语法角度看是同等重要的,这显然违背了原句的核心。

对这样的一个句子,如果我们知道现在分词结构放在句子后面(注意,句子后面要接现在分词时,必须在分词前加上逗号),可以表达句子内容产生的结果,那么,本句就可以写成下面这样:

Mary dislikes English, making her mom angry.

别看这个小小的改动,它把原句存在的几个问题统统解决了,同时 making 的使用又符合现在分词的用法之一。另外,改动后的句子采用的是句子加分词短语的形式,非常符合现代英文对句子结构的要求。

同样,我们看一个类似的句子:

The asteroid impacted on the earth and it caused the extinction of dinosaur.

这个句子和刚才的句子存在同样的问题。首先是 it 的使用问题,再就是 and 不能用来连接因果关系的句子,同时句子也存在主次内容不分的问题,如果改成一个句子加现在分词的结构就把所有的问题解决了。可以改为:

The asteroid impacted on the earth, causing the extinction of dinosaur.

我们把现在分词的一些典型用法归类如下，大家在英文写作时遇到相关概念可优先考虑使用。使用现在分词结构，不仅可以简化句子，更主要的是能使句子的中心意思更加突出，结构更清楚明了。

现在分词用在句子的最前面，表示：

时间

例：When I travelled in Moscow, I met many Russian friends.

使用现在分词结构，可以改为：

(When) travelling in Moscow, I met many Russian friends.

例：While I was taking a shower, I heard the telephone ringing.

可以改为：(While) taking a shower, I heard the telephone ringing.

（注意，当原句的连词是 when 或 while 的时候，简化后 when 和 while 可以保留也可以不保留。）

例：After I finished my homework, I went to sleep.

可以改为：After finishing my homework, I went to sleep. (after 必须保留)

例：After I had finished my homework, I went to sleep.

可以改为：Having finished my homework, I went to sleep.

（注意，原句是 had done 或 have done 的结构时，现在分词要采用 having done 的形式。）

原因

现在分词置于句首，可以表达原因，那么原句中的一些表原因的连词如 because、since 等就可以省略了。

例：Because I know Mary well, I lent her 1,000 dollars.

可以改为：Knowing Mary well, I lent her 1,000 dollass.

例：Since we could not reach a compromise, we have to resort to legal procedures.

可以改为：Not finding a compromise, we have to resort to legal procedures.

例：Because she has just recovered from her recent illness, she needs time to adjust herself.

可以改为：Having just recovered from her recent illness, she needs time to adjust herself.

伴随动作

例： Singing a song, the teacher entered the classroom.

在这个例句中，句子的主要动作 entered 和 singing 是同时发生的，所以把次要动作 sing 作为分词形式放在句首，表示 enter 的伴随动作。

同样，看下面几个用现在分词表示伴随动作的例句：

Smiling affectionately, my mom eyed me with satisfaction.

Picking the newspaper, the businessman stood up to walk to the window.

Flicking cigarette lighter, the bodyguard approached the girl's table.

在实际运用中，现在分词还常常放在一个句子的后面，在这种情况下，现在分词表示以下的特定含意：

伴随动作

在刚才提到现在分词表示伴随动作的四个例句中，现在分词部分可以放到句子的后面。

例： The teacher entered the classroom, singing a song.

My mom eyed me with satisfaction, smiling affectionately.

The businessman stood up to walk to the window, picking the newspaper.

The bodyguard approached the girl's table, flicking cigarette lighter.

表示句子的动作产生的结果

例： Mary dislikes English, making her mom angry.

The plane inadvertently crashed on the building, causing 7 deaths and 3 injuries.

My father lost his job in the financial storm, leaving us in a difficult situation.

以上三个句子，逗号后的现在分词结构都是逗号前面句子的谓语动作产生的结果。

为句子的内容提供进一步的信息或解释

例： She studied English hard, immersing herself in reading English novels. （用现在分词 immersing 表示她是如何努力学习英文的）

Uday Hussein loathed the sunlight, working at night and sleeping during the day.

The coach punished the players regularly, shaving off the eyebrows of those who displeased him. （用现在分词 shaving off 对教练惩罚运动员进行进一步解释。）

综上所述，正是具有许多独特的功能和含意，现在分词在当代英文中被广泛运用。使用现在分词不仅可以简化句子，更重要的是可以使句子结构更加清楚紧凑，句子重心更加突出。

第六节　学会简化从句

在写英文作文时,我们当然离不开从句,但在一个完整的句子里过多地使用从句,会使句子凌乱复杂,使读者的记忆不堪重负。同时,由于许多同学驾驭句子结构的能力有限,如果在一个完整的句子里包括了太多的从句,而又不会正确地处理,则往往会使句子重心不突出,同时造成句意混乱。

中式英文有一个很大的特点是动不动就用复杂句(即一个主句加一个或以上的从句形式),这主要还是因为写作者的中式思维造成的。我们看下面一个句子,这个冗长得让人难以忍受的句子里包括了太多的从句,而这些从句大多是不必要的。

例: A girl who is three year old got hurt because when she was playing on a slide she slipped from the slide and got hurt in her left leg by a screw which was put in the slide by one of the workers who worked in the park.

相信很多读者读完这个句子,要是中途不换气的话,估计都憋死了。这个冗长的复杂句包括了太多从句及一些毫无必要的信息和重复信息。其实作者要传达的信息很简单,就是一个小女孩的左腿被公园滑梯上的一个钉子伤了。看看简化后的句子:

A three-year old girl got hurt in her left leg by a screw in the slide when she was playing in the park.

例: I love the book which is written by that famous novelist.

这个句子里的 which is 是纯属多余,不如删掉。删掉后,原来的复杂句就变成简单句加过去分词的结构,简洁明了而不失原意。

英文中的从句可以归为三类,每一类从句的简化都有其固定形式,分别介绍如下:

定语从句的简化

定语从句指的是一个句子修饰前面的某个名词,对该名词进行限定修饰,如 I love the book <u>which is written by that famous novelist</u>,这个句子中的划线部分就是个定语从句，由 which 引导，对 book 进行限定。定语从句的简化分为以下两种情况。

a. 当从句中有 be 动词时，直接去掉连词和 be 动词，而不管 be 动词后的成分。

Do you know the boy **who is** playing there?

→ Do you know the boy playing there?

The man **who is** standing at the gate is my boyfriend.

→ The man standing at the gate is my boyfriend.

Books **which are** written in English are more expensive.

→ Books written in English are more expensive.

Those people **who are** responsible for the incident were all punished.

→ Those people responsible for the incident were all punished.

Scientists are especially interested in the bird **which is** native to Congo.

→ Scientists are especially interested in the bird native to Congo.

b. 当从句中没有 be 动词时，去掉连词并把动词变成"V-ing"形式

They live in a room **that faces** the south.

→ They live in a room facing the south.

Anyone **who touches** the wire will get an electric shock.

→ Anyone touching the wire will get an electric shock.

English has an alphabet **that consists** of 26 letters.

→ English has an alphabet consisting of 26 letters.

注意：只有在连接代词做从句的主语时，定语从句才能按上述原则进行简化。

I like the book which you are reading.

这个定语从句不能简化，因为连接代词 which 不是定语从句的主语。

I like the book which contains pictures.

这个定语从句可以简化为 I like the book containing pictures，因为连接代词 which 同时又做定语从句的主语。

名词从句的简化

所谓的名词从句，就是从句的性质和功能相当于一个名词，做另外一个句子的相应的成分（如主语或宾语等），并据此划分为主语从句、宾语从句、同位语从句和表语从句四种。

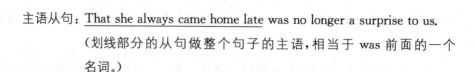

主语从句：<u>That she always came home late</u> was no longer a surprise to us.

（划线部分的从句做整个句子的主语，相当于 was 前面的一个名词。）

宾语从句：She insisted <u>that I should apologize to her.</u>

（划线部分相当于 insist 的宾语，由连词 that 引导。）

表语从句：The book was <u>what she was most interested in.</u>

（划线部分是相当于整个句子的表语。注意，凡是 be 动词后的从句就叫表语从句。）

同位语从句：The news <u>that her son died in the battle</u> was the last straw in camel for that old woman.

（同位语从句，就是整个句子对前面的一个名词进行内容上的解释。在该句中，划线部分是对 news 的内容进行解释，所以划线部分是个同位语从句。）

以上四种名词从句，都可以简化成短语的形式，现将其基本简化规则介绍如下：

a. that 引导的主语从句可以简化为 sb's doing。

<u>That John won the race</u> surprised us.

→ John's winning the race surprised us.

<u>That he lost the game</u> came as a surprise to everyone.

→ His losing the game came as a surprise to everyone.

b. that 引导的同位语从句可以简化为"of ＋动名词"的复合结构。

There was no chance <u>that Davy would come from the battle alive.</u>

→ There was no chance of Davy's coming from the battle alive.

I don't think the statement that <u>the economic recovery would be just around the corner</u> is true.

→ I don't think the statement of economic recovery's just being around the corner is true.

c. that 引导的宾语从句，可以简化为动名词或动词不定式。这要取决于动词的性质。

I hope <u>that</u> I can drive to work in my own car.

→ I <u>hope to</u> drive to work in my own car.

I consider <u>that</u> I will immigrate to America in the future.

→ I <u>consider immigrating</u> to America in the future.

在有些动词后还要加介词（preposition）。

Jane's mother insisted that she should go swimming with her brother.

→ Jane's mother <u>insisted on</u> her going swimming with her brother.

状语从句的简化

状语从句用来表述主句发生的时间、地点、原因、结果、目的、条件、方式等。只有状语从句的主语和主句的主语相同时，状语从句才能简化，否则句意改变，出现悬垂错误。

例：While the teacher was lecturing to the class，I fell asleep.

在这个句子里，由于状语从句的主语(the teacher)和主句的主语(I)不同，所以该状语从句不能简化。

例：While I was driving on the road，a cat suddenly jumped out of the forest.

同样，在这个句子里，因为状语从句的主语(I)和主句的主语(a cat)不同，所以该状语从句不能简化，如果非要按我们下面的规则简化，则是：

While driving on the road，a cat suddenly jumped out of the forest.

而这个句子的中文意思是，当猫在路上驾驶的时候，它从森林里跑了出来，显然不合逻辑。

状语从句的简化按下面的规则：

a. 从句中含有 be 动词时，省去从句的主语和 be 动词。

Metals expand when <u>they are</u> heated and contract when <u>they are</u> cooled.

→ Metals expand when heated and contract when cooled.

When <u>he was</u> a student，he read a lot.

→ When a student，he read a lot.

While <u>I was</u> waiting，I took out a magazine to read.

→ While waiting，I took out a magazine to read.

A tiger can't be tamed unless <u>it is</u> caught young.

→ A tiger can't be tamed unless caught young.

Although <u>he was</u> not an economist himself，Dr. Smith has long been a severe critic of the government's economic policy.

→ Although not an economist himself，Dr. Smith has long been a severe critic of the government's economic policy.

b. 当从句中没有 be 动词时，去掉从句主语，并将动词变为"V-ing"形式。

Since I came to Vancouver, I have made many new friends.

→ Since coming to Vancouver, I have made many new friends.

After I finished my homework, I fed the dog.

→ After finishing my homework, I fed the dog.

After I had finished my homework, I fed the dog.

→ After having finished my homework, I fed the dog. (注意，从句中的 have done 或 had done,简化后要写成 having done,而不能是 doing)

第七节　典型从句的变化处理

在上一节里，我们谈到三类从句的简化，这一节，我们谈谈几类典型从句的变化问题。这几类从句都是学生作文里经常出现的，且都是可以通过各种方式改进的。不是说我们不能使用从句，而是在一篇作文里，如果写作者能对一些从句进行变化处理，可以使句式更加多样化，增加文章的可读性，避免单调乏味的通病。

1. 对 if 类从句的变化处理

中式英文的一个特点就是大量使用 if 条件从句，这可能和我们中文里喜欢说"如果"有关系。许多写作者一旦在脑子里出现"如果"这两个字，第一反应就是要使用 if，事实上，if 条件句在很多情况下都是可以避免的。

例1：如果你没有通过考试，大学会让你暂停学习。

中式英文：If you fail to pass the exam, the college will have to suspend you.

许多同学的脑子里一旦出现上述的中文概念就会立即写出上面的中式英文来。不是说这样写就一定有问题，但下面的一个简单句不仅保留了原意，而且减少了原来句子的对抗性。

例2：Failure to pass the exam may result in suspension by college.

原句使用 you，虽然这个 you 可能指所有人，但 you 的使用总是让读者觉得很不舒服，整个句子的火药味也很浓。改动后的句子把意思表达到位了，又避免使用 you，减少了句子的对抗性，同时把原来的一个复杂句改为了简单句。

例3：If you break the law, you may be arrested.

这个句子存在的问题和上面的例子一样，但如果改为下面的简单句形式，则漂亮很多：

Anyone breaking the law may end up being arrested.

Anyone breaking the law may be arrested.

再看几个 if 条件从句的变化处理。

例4：If words are taken out of context, they are not very likely to mean the same as they do when they are in context.

→Words taken out of context don not always mean what they do in context. If we want to end a war, we must lose it.

→The quickest way to end a war is to lose it.

例 5：If you imitate others, you can never expect to be a great novelist.

→No one can expect to be a great novelist by imitation.

例 6：If a teacher uses verbal abuses or threats to make his students perform well on study, these measures may not produce desirable result.

→Verbal abuses or threats by a teacher may not produce desirable result on the part of the students.

例 7：When a Chinese writer describes the Sahara desert, he says if you want to know what "fear" means, you have to cross it.

→Describing the Sahara desert, a Chinese writer said to cross it is to know fear. （改动后的句子巧妙使用 to do something is to do something 的结构。）

例 8：If the government intervenes, the prices will stop increasing, and that is the only way to decrease the price.

→The only way to combat increased price is through government intervention.

例 9：If weather permits, we will go out for a picnic next Sunday.

→Weather permitting, we will go out for a picnic next Sunday.

（把原句的 if 从句变成了一个独立主格形式,这样,原来的复杂句就变成了一个简单句）

2. 对 because 从句的变化处理

because 从句是一个经常被滥用的句子。在表达原因的四个连词中(另外 3 个是 since、for 和 as),写作者最喜欢用的还是 because。只要句子是谈原因的,大部分写作者都会采用 because 来引导从句。其实,because 引导的从句表达的原因往往是一个强烈的原因,或是别人所不知道的原因。一个众所周知的原因,或一个不需要强调的原因往往用 since 来引导,这是大家应该首先要注意的。因此,because 从句用得不好,就带有点侮辱性了。

例1：Because tomorrow is Saturday，we will have one day off.

这个句子用 because 引导，其潜台词是，说话者认为听话者不知道明天是周六，这显然是有点侮辱性了。所以，还是把 because 改为 since 比较妥当。

其实，很多时候可以避免使用 because 从句。因为我们在写作中，即使在写纯粹说理性的文章时，也没有那么多强烈的原因要表达。以下是一些 because 从句的改进：

例2：Because I have been very busy recently，I am afraid that I can't go to your birthday party.

→I am afraid that I can't go to your birthday party due to my busy schedule.（把 because 从句变成了一个简单的名词结构。）

例3：China began to implement the policy of family planning and because of that it has successfully curbed the rapid increase of population.

→China began to implement the policy of family planning 30 years ago, thus curbing the rapid increase of population.（把 because 从句变成了现在分词结构，表示主句产生的结果，这也符合现在分词的用法。）

例4：Just because subscription price has come down does not mean that circulation will go up.

→The drop in subscription price does not necessarily mean the increase of circulation.（把原句的复杂句变成了简单句，避免了 because 从句的使用。）

例5：Because he lacks strong evident to support his argument，the author does not succeed in making a convincing case for curbing the family violence.

→Lacking strong evident to support his argument，the author fail to make a convincing case for curbing the family violence.（把原句的 because 从句变成了表示原因的现在分词结构，这也符合现在分词置于句首的用法。）

例6：Because Brian didn't have sufficient financial backing, he failed to complete his college study.

→Brian's limited financial backing prevented him from completing his college study.（把原句的 because 从句改成了一个名词结构，同时使用了 prevent somebody from doing something 这一地道英文结构。)

3. 对 but 从句的变化处理

许多 but 从句都是可以避免的,从而使原句变成一个简单句。这不仅使得原句更为简洁,更主要的是使 but 前后的两个句子更加紧密。

例 1：The room was silent，but suddenly there was a thunder outside.

→The silence of the room was broken by a sudden thunder outside.

→A sudden thunder outside terminated the silence of the room.

(原句中的 but 没有把两个句子的内在联系表达出来,改动后的两个句子都是简单句,把原句的内在联系体现出来了。)

例 2：The book is about a young athlete，but it is more than just that.

→The book is more that just about a young athlete.

(省去 but 把原句改为一个简单句。)

例 3：My son was adroit at many computer games，but I have never played them.

→My son was adroit at many computer games that I have never played.

(把原句的 but 从句改成了一个定语从句。)

例 4：As a young man，he tried many different things，but he hardly succeeded in any one of them at the beginning.

→As a young man，he tried many different things，all with little initial success. (这一句的修改非常成功,把 but 从句改成了一个非常地道的 all with 独立结构,使句子更加简洁,重心突出。)

例 5：Music lightens life，but literature deepens it.

→Music lightens life；literature deepens it.

(将 but 改为分号,以增加前后两个句子的对比关系。)

例 6：It is not his capability but his attitude that results in his dismissal.

→His attitude，not his capability，results in his dismissal.

(修改后的句子语气更强了,意思表达更直接。)

4. 对 so 从句的变化处理

So 从句常常表达主句的结果，同时和 that 联合表达目的和结果。我们看下面的例句是如何避免 so 从句的。

例 1：I want to travel in Europe next year, so I am now working part time in a restaurant.

→I am now working part time in a restaurant for a trip to Europe next year.

（改动后的句子把原来的从句内容变成了主句，这也符合这句话本来的意思。英文喜欢先说你在干什么，再接着说为什么要这么干。）

例 2：McDonald is so popular in china that, like Coca Cola, it has become a household name.

→McDonald, like Coca Cola, is a household name in China.

（一个简单的 like 结构，避免使用原句的 so ... that 句型。）

例 3：The word list is formatted alphabetically so that it is easy for the reader to use.

→The word list is formatted alphabetically for reader's ease of use.

（使用名词结构替换一个从句，这点非常值得我们学习。我们在写作时候动不动就喜欢用从句，但事实上，这些带有中文痕迹的从句很多都可以用一个名词结构表示。）

例 4：She was sleeping like a log that nothing I did could wake him up.

→Nothing I did could wake her up form her sound sleep.

（也是用一个名词结构表达从句的内容。）

例 5：Many people in Shanghai used to live in attics, so they could see only a blank wall surrounding them.

→Many people in Shanghai used to live in attics, with only a blank wall at sight. （改动后的句子非常地道，非常符合英文的表达习惯。）

例 6：The writing guide is such an indispensable book that anyone who wants to write professionally should possess one.

→ The writing guide is indispensable for anyone who wants to write professionally.

　　上述四类从句经常被学生滥用，它们也是中式英文的一种表现形式。不是说我们不能使用这些从句，而是为同学们提供了另外的一些表达方式。我们在写作的时候有必要思考一下，对于一个想要表达的意思，是不是非要从句不可呢，是不是还有更好的表达方式可以绕开从句呢？相对于一个结构来说，从句不仅显得啰嗦，还会冲淡句子的核心意思，这也是为什么现代英文偏好句子加短语的表达方式。

第八节 句子的合并

对一个初学英文的写作者来说,如果掌握了基本的造句知识,具备基础的语法知识和一定的词汇量,要写出一个简单句不会有太大的问题。但是文章中充斥着太多的简单句,会让人觉得该写作者语言稚嫩,思想不成熟。同时,这些简单句之间本身存在着一定的语义逻辑,但是这些逻辑被句号强行割断了。

因此,我们有必要对一些有着内在联系的简单句进行合并。合并后的句子往往是一个复合句或复杂句,或者是一个简单句加上各式各样的短语形式。

例 1:Moby Dick is a book. It is a long book. It is about a whale. A man named Ahab tries to kill it. Herman Melville wrote it.

这 5 个简单句的句子本身并没有错,但是,它们之间存在一定的联系,应该合并成一个完整的句子:

Herman Melville wrote a long book called Moby Dick, which is the story of the struggle of a man against a whale.

合并后的句子调顺了原来 5 个简单句的先后关系,其中包含一个过去分词结构及一个定语从句。同时,故事的内容用 struggle of a man against a whale 这样的表达,要比原句(A man named Ahab tries to kill it)的表达更丰富,原句关于故事内容的表达仅仅用 kill,把故事情节简单化了。

例 2:People change and places change as well. Jennifer felt this strongly. She had been away for eleven years.

这 3 个简单句存在内部的逻辑关系,但是被句号分割开了。三个句子的时间顺序也存在问题,应该是先说 Jennifer 离开 11 年后回来这件事,再说她回来的感受,但原句没有把这个顺序体现出来,所以使读者感到跳跃性很大,不能立即把握作者的真实意图。修改如下:

On returning after an eleven-year absence, Jennifer had a strong feeling of how people and places change.

修改后的句子体现了正确的时间及逻辑关系,而且用 absence 把 had been away 的意思表达出来了,符合英文表达的简洁性原则,即能用一个单词表达的,绝不用一个句子来表达。

例 3: She was walking aimlessly in the forest. Her dog was following her.

这两个句子也是存在内在联系的。她在森林里漫无目的地走路是核心,伴随动作是小狗跟在后面。两个简单句应该合并成如下一个句子:

She was walking aimlessly in the forest, her dog following her.

合并后的句子变成了一个句子加上一个独立主格的结构。

例 4: I got up at seven in the morning. It is a beautiful morning. The birds were singing happily in the trees.

→I got up at seven in a beautiful morning when the birds were singing happing in the trees.

例 5: My name is Connie Law. I am seventeen. I am a girl and I am a student. I am now studying in a high school.

→My name is Connie Law, and I am a student of seventeen who is now studying in a high school.

例 6: Beijing streets are crowded with taxis, company cars and private vehicles owned by the newly affluent. The number has been rising rapidly in the last few years. The latest statistics show there are now 1. 2 million vehicles in Beijing alone.

→Taxi, company car and private vehicle owned by the newly affluent have crammed Beijing streets in rising numbers in the last few years-1. 2 million vehicles at last count.

例 7: His is a wreck. It was formerly the stately Imperial Garden. It is preserved deliberately as a reminder and symbol.

→This wreck, formerly the stately Imperial Garden, is preserved deliberately as a reminder and symbol. (巧妙使用同位语结构,把三个简单句合并成了一个句子,使得句意更加紧凑。)

例 8: Mary graduated last summer. He joined the General Motor in New York soon after graduation. He received an engineering degree from his college.

→After graduating last summer with an engineering degree, Mary soon joined General Motor in New York. (原句的时间顺序混乱,修改后的句子把正确的时间

顺序体现出来了。)

例 9：I have always had a dream. My dream has been to be a famous writer. Everyone would read my books. I would become very wealthy.

→ I have always dreamed of becoming a wealthy and famous writer read by everyone. （修改后的句子把原来几个简单句用几个单词就表达出来了。）

例 10：It was quite obvious at that time that IQ equals intelligence. Since them, however, many people have seriously criticized the idea.

→The idea that IQ equals intelligence seemed obvious at the time but has since come under much criticism. （使用一个同位语从句把本来有联系的两个简单句合并成为一个句子。）

例 11：She sat there thinking hard about her future. She did not say anything at the same time.

→Speechless, she sat there thinking hard about her future. （使用一个独立形容词结构把两个句子合并成一个句子。speechless 描写她在思考时的状态，以代替 she did not say anything at the same time 这个简单句，使句意更加紧凑。）

例 12：The native looked at us with suspicion. He was holding a spear in his hand.

→The native looked us with suspicion, holding a spear in his hand. （利用现在分词可以表示伴随动作的特点，把两个简单句合并成一个简单句加短语的形式。）

例 13：The father was furious. He demanded to see the daughter's boyfriend himself.

→Furious, the father demanded to see the daughter's boyfriend himself. （使用独立形容词结构将两个简单句合并。同时，去掉了干扰核心词汇（father 和 furious)的一些词，使 furious 这一状态形容词更加突出。）

例 14：She said that she could not do it for us. So, we would have to find other candidates.

→Since she said she could not do it for us, we would have to find other candidates. （把原来两个有联系的简单句合并成表示原因的状语从句加主句的形式，使因果关系得到更好的体现。）

例 15： The auditorium is across the park. It is a gift of the alumni.

→ The auditorium, across the park, is a gift of the alumni. （使用介词词组，把两个句子合并成一个带有同位语结构的简单句。）

以上十几个例句旨在抛砖引玉，给大家一点启发。把几个简单句合并成一个紧凑的句子，需要很多技巧及扎实的英文功底。同学们要在平时多看多读，更主要的是要学会欣赏漂亮的句子，多从报刊杂志上收集素材，并在自己的习作中加以运用。慢慢地，你驾驭句子的能力就在潜移默化中提高了。

第九节　学会转化词性

在第二节里,我们谈到关于动词使用的问题。其中讲到,现在英文中,许多名词甚至副词和数词都可以转化为动词,从而增加文字的生动性。这一节我们谈谈不同词性的单词之间的性质转化,这种转化有时候起到使句意简洁的作用,有时候使表达更加贴切,更加符合地道英文的表达习惯。

例 1：The couple was deserted on the island and they could find nobody there.

→The couple was deserted on the island, <u>with nobody in sight</u>. （弱化 they could find nobody 这一事实,因为被 deserted on the island 是主要事实,后面的内容只是补充,所以使用并列句不合适。）

例 2：To get a closer look at the bothers Hussein, TIME interviewed dozens of sources which know well the two men, including butlers, maids, bodyguards and friends.

→ To get a closer look at the bothers Hussein, TIME interviewed dozens of sources <u>with knowledge of</u> the two men, including butlers, maids, bodyguards and friends. （我们一说"知道什么"就用 which（或 who）knows something,地道的英文说 with the knowledge of something。）

例 3：The company was pleased to embrace the new years by announcing that it had <u>merged</u> a new company specialized in computer games software.

→ The company was pleased to embrace the new years by announcing <u>the merge of</u> a new company specialized in computer games software. （把原来的从句改成了一个名词短语,merge 既可以做动词也可以做名词。）

例 4：The fact that the murderer was himself tortured by her husband did not <u>provide any justification</u> for her atrocious act.

→ The fact that the murderer was himself tortured by her husband did not <u>justify</u> her atrocious act. （用动词 justify 要比用 provide justification 更简洁更地道。）

例 5：When I <u>saw</u> my teacher in his rags on the street, I was shocked: how decent he was 20 years ago when he taught my biology.

→The <u>sight</u> of my teacher in his rags on the street shocked me: how decent he was 20 years ago when he taught my biology.（我们表达"看见"这个意思往往用 see,其实,用名词 sight 也是个很不错的选择。）

例 6：The smog <u>suffocated</u> people and it is turning away tourists

→The <u>suffocating</u> smog turns away tourists.（把动词 suffocate 直接改成形容词 suffocating 修饰 smog,强化 turn away 的动作。）

例 7：Once your have <u>completed</u> the forms, please submit it to the receptionist.

→The <u>completed</u> forms should go to the receptionist.（修改后的句子更符合英文的表达习惯。动词 complete 采用过去分词 completed 的形式,使句子的主要意思更加突出。）

例 8：I would especially <u>thank</u> Mr. Brian for his consistent support throughout these years.

→ My special <u>thanks</u> go to Mr. Brian for his consistent support throughout these years.（把动词 thank 变成名词 thanks。想想奥斯卡颁奖典礼上那些获奖者是怎么说的,就明白改动后的句子是多么地道了。）

例 9：In Qing Emperor's eyes, building the Great Wall is the best way to <u>defend</u> the country from outside invasion.

→ In Qing Emperor's eyes, building the Great Wall is the best <u>defence</u> against outside invasion.（把动词 defend 变成名词 defence,省去了无关紧要的 the way。）

例 10：The reasoning contains <u>flaws</u> in two important respects.

→The reasoning is <u>flawed</u> in two important respects.（把名词 flaw 用作动词,更符合英文的表达习惯。）

例 11：The English writing instructor asks the students to write their essays <u>in double space</u>.

→ The English writing instructor asks the students to <u>double space</u> their essays.（double space 在改动后的句子被用成动词形式。）

例 12：Mom <u>used a spoon</u> to scoop up a little salt and put it into the soup.

→Mom <u>spooned</u> a little salt into the soup.（把名词 spoon 用作动词，多么地道，多么简洁！）

例 13：The peers were repulsed by his behaviour <u>which is typical of a lady</u>.

→The peers were repulsed by his <u>lady-like</u> behaviour.（用一个形容词解决了一个从句要表达的意思。）

例 14：The current problem should be solved <u>in a quick way</u>.

→ The current problem should be solved <u>quickly</u>.（quickly 就很好，为什么要用这么累赘的 in a quick way?）

例 15：Churchill married rather late，at 33，was lucky in his wife，and has lived in <u>monogamous happy marriage</u> ever since.

→ Churchill married rather late，at 33，was lucky in his wife，and has lived in <u>monogamous happiness</u> ever since.（monogamous 本身就有婚姻的意思了，所以原句的 marriage 是多余的，把形容词 happy 变成名词 happiness，就把这个问题解决了。）

例 16：We applied green <u>paint</u> to the ceiling.

→We <u>painted</u> the ceiling green.（中文说"涂上油漆"，所以到英文里自然就说 apply the paint 了，为什么不直接把 paint 用作动词呢？）

例 17：The police are <u>conducting a thorough investigation</u> into the case.

→The police are thoroughly <u>investigating</u> into the case.（中文说"进行调查，"许多同学总是要把"进行"给表达出来，所以就用了 conduct，但英文应该直接用动词 investigate。请记住，在 SAT 中，动词的使用优先于名词的使用。这句话的核心动作是 investigate，而不是 conduct。）

例 18：His friends are doubtful <u>whether it is wise</u> for him to marry such a prodigal girl.

→His friends are doubtful of his <u>wisdom</u> of marrying such a prodigal girl. （whether it is 加形容词的结构被用得太滥了，改动后的句子用一个名词 wisdom，多么简洁，多么直截了当啊。）

例 19：I was struck by the fact that this town did not change a bit in the course of time.

→I was stuck by the timelessness of the town. （一个 timelessness 就把一个从句的意思表达得很到位了。）

例 20：His contribution to the final victory of the team was <u>noticed</u> by many students.

→His contribution to the final victory of the team <u>didn't go unnoticed</u> by many students. （把动词 notice 变成 not go unnoticed，起到了强调的作用，也符合英文的表达习惯。）

例 21：He <u>nodded</u> his head to <u>acknowledge</u> that he <u>failed</u>.

→His <u>nodding</u> is an <u>acknowledgement</u> of his <u>failure</u>. （三个改变，一个是把动词 nod 改成名词性质的 nodding，二是把动词 acknowledge 变成名词 acknowledgement，最后就是把动词 failed 改成名词 failure。改动后避免了从句。其实，原句不一定不好，只是多了一种表达方式而已。）

例 22：The nurse looked at the <u>newborn baby</u> with affection.

→The nurse looked at the <u>newborn</u> with affection. （newborn 也可以作名词用，是新生儿的意思。改动后的句子把原句形容词性质的 newborn 变成名词性质。）

第十节　学会使用无偏见英语

　　语言是现实的一面镜子,语言必然会反映社会生活的方方面面。按《圣经》的说法,上帝首先创造的是男人(亚当),而女人(夏娃)是男人身上的一根肋骨造的,所以,女人依附男人而存在。这个根深蒂固的基督教思想,反映到英语里,就是有大量性别歧视性的文字。比如,man 这个词,既可指"男人",又可指代"人类",完全忽视了女人也是人类重要的一半。同样,当我们无法知道一个对象的性别时,就用 he, him 或 his 来代替,这也是含有性别歧视的英文单词。另外,有很多表示职业的名词是以 man 为后缀的,尽管从事这些职业的有很多女性,比如中文里的董事长在英文里就叫 chairman,尽管这个 chairman 可能是个 woman。

　　自上个世纪 70 年代以来,西方的女权运动开始兴起。受到这一社会思潮的影响,女权主义者掀起了一场旨在消除性别歧视的文字变革运动,对当代英文产生了深远的影响,也创造了许多无性别偏见的英文单词,最典型的就是 Ms. 这个单词。英语中,对男子的称呼一律是 Mr. ,这个词看不出这个男人是否结婚,而对未婚的女人称 Miss,对已婚的女人就称 Mrs,这让女权主义者感到不悦。为什么男子不分已婚未婚,只有 Mr 这个词,而女子却要分已婚的 Mrs 和未婚的 Miss 呢? 女权主义者认为这便是男女不平等,于是便造了 Ms,对已婚未婚女子一律通用,与 Mr 分庭抗礼。现在大家都对 Ms 这一称呼习以为常了。

　　我们在英文习作中,要尽量避免使用带有性别歧视的单词,特别对 SAT 作文来说,如果阅卷者恰恰就是个狂热的女权运动者,而你的作文中出现性别歧视的词汇,这多多少少会影响一个阅卷者对你的作文的印象。事实上,有很多办法可以避免使用带有性别歧视的单词。

1. 在泛指时候,尽量使用复数名词或 one,以避免使用 he 或 him

例 1：An excellent student should finish <u>his</u> homework timely.

→Excellent students should finish <u>their</u> homework timely.

例 2：A competent news reporter should be able to handle <u>his</u> material on a fair and objective basis.

→Competent news reporter should be able to handle <u>their</u> material on a fair and objective basis.

例 3：A college graduate seeking employment should mention <u>his or her</u> educational background in his or her resumes

→ College graduates seeking employment should mention <u>their</u> educational backgrounds in their resumes.（原句的 his or her 虽然没有性别歧视的问题，但是实在太啰嗦了，特别是在一篇文章里，如果用太多的 his or her 就会太累赘，使用复数名词就把这个问题解决了。）

2. 在表示泛指时候，可以使用被动语态或设法绕过人称代词

例 1：The receptionist urges each candidate to finish his application form before 5 o'clock.

→The receptionist urges each candidate that the application form should be finished before 5 o'clock.

例 2：Just a musician has to be a master of his or her instrument，a writer is at his or her best when he or she has mastered his or her linguistic tools.

→Mastery of words is as important to a writer as mastery of an instrument is to a musician.

例 3：A pilot should offer his advice during an emergency.

→Advice should be offered by a pilot during an emergency.

3. 避免使用 man 称谓泛称或带有 man 结尾的单词

例 1：Judy was excited to learn that she had been appointed the chairman of the company.

→Judy was excited to learn that she had been appointed the chairperson of the company.

例 2：Becoming a policeman has been Carolyn's dream since her childhood.

→Becoming a police officer has been Carolyn's dream since her childhood.

例 3：The boss was trying to figure out who would be the best <u>man</u> for the job.

→ The boss was trying to figure out who would be the best <u>person</u>（or: employee）for the job.

例 4：It is true that <u>man</u> is liable to see the imperfection of others than of his own.

→It is true that <u>we</u> are liable to see the imperfection of others than of our own.

例 5：The new <u>spokesman</u> for the Ministry of Foreign Affairs is really eloquent.

→The new <u>spokesperson</u> for the Ministry of Foreign Affairs is really eloquent.

例 6：The <u>postman</u> handled his material carefully.

→The <u>mailperson</u> handled the mail carefully.

4. 不要刻意强调性别差异

就传统来说，一些带有专业性质的工作往往都是男人的专利，但随着社会发展，这些工作领域也不乏女性的身影，可是人们习惯上总是喜欢在这些工作岗位前面加上个 woman 或 female。比如一个国家的总统是女的，人们总会说 Do you know the female president in that country？事实上，这句话本身就是性别歧视了，好像女人当总统多么让人大惊小怪似的。

例 1：Two <u>woman</u> representatives will be serving you right away.

→Two representatives will be serving you right away.

例 2：The <u>woman</u> doctor is a film buff.

→The doctor is a film buff.

一般来讲，你在作文中用 he 代替所有人，应该问题不大，但万一碰到阅卷者是个女权主义者，那么她多少会有一些不舒服。所以，还是尽量使用无偏见词语为妥。

第十一节 演绎法和归纳法的写作方式

在英文写作中，段落是一篇作文的重要组成部分。一般来说，一个段落应该包括一个 topic sentence，几句支持 topic sentence 的句子以及一个结束句即 concluding sentence。虽然写作时不是每一段都要这么写，但一篇标准议论文的段落是应该具备上述要素的。

在段落写作上，有两种方式可以运用，一种是演绎法（deductive method），另外一种是归纳法（inductive method）。这两种方式到底有什么区别呢？

简单来说，演绎法就是先说一个一般的结论，然后由这个结论推到一些具体的相关个体事件；而归纳法恰恰相反，它是从一些具体的论据中推出一个一般的结论，就是说先提出相关论据，然后得出结论。

看下面的例子：

Mary studies hard and is always there to help her classmates with her homework. In her spare time, she does volunteering in a community center on a regular basis. She also devotes her time to helping her mother with house chores. In many ways, Mary is a model student.

这一段是个典型的归纳法范例。先说了 Mary 的一些表现，最后得出结论：Mary 是个模范学生。本段先提出论据，由这些论据得出了结论。

In many ways, Mary is a model student. Mary studies hard and is always there to help her classmates with her homework. In her spare time, she does volunteering in a community center on a regular basis. She also devotes her time to helping her mother with house chores.

这一段是典型的演绎法范例。先给出结论说 Mary 是个模范学生，接着举例来证明她为什么是个好学生。

在英文写作特别是议论文写作上，宜采用演绎法的方式来展开一个段落甚至一篇文章的写作。使用演绎法的好处是，作者把自己的观点首先向读者表明，让读者心中有数，然后再给读者提供各种论据以证明自己的观点，这样整篇文章的结构就非常清楚。如果采用归纳法，因为读者事先并不知道作者的论点，仅仅看论据，就难免会自己猜测，有时候会导致读者不明白作者到底要证明什么样的观点。事先让读者知道自己的观点，等于读者有了个方向，接下来就是要顺着作者的文字，去看作者讲的观点是否得到充分支持。

最不能接受的就是有些写作者在写作时，把演绎法和归纳法混合使用，这样会给读者造成很大的理解障碍。

我们看下面的一段作文，讲的都是同一个内容，但由于采用了不同的写作方式，使它们各自的清晰度差别很大。

Paragraph A

(1) The country has rich, modern cities with towering buildings, eight-lane highways and luxurious shopping centres. (2) On the other hand, there is the poor countryside, where people have retained their traditional lifestyle. (3) A stark contrast can clearly be observed between the cities and the countryside. (4) The rich are separated from the poor, and, correspondingly, the modern from the traditional. (5) The country is thus marked by two major, related socio-economic divisions.

【点评】

这是一个典型的归纳法写作方式，前面4句话都是论据，结论是第五句即结束句。

Paragraph B

(1) The country is marked by two major, related socio-economic divisions. (2) The first is between the rich and the poor, while the second is a corresponding division between the modern and the traditional. (3) These distinctions can clearly be observed in the contrast between the cities and the countryside. (4) The great wealth and modernity of the cities with their towering buildings, eight-lane highways and luxurious shopping centers offer a stark contrast with the poverty and traditional life of the countryside.

【点评】

这是个典型的演绎法写作方式。作者首先提出结论，第二句是把结论的具体内容进一步细化，而第三和第四句都是支持结论，属于论据。我们在SAT作文中应该尽量采用这样的写作方式。

Paragraph C

(1) The rich of the country are separated from the poor, and, correspondingly, the modern from the traditional. (2) The country is thus marked by two major,

related socio-economic divisions. （3） There are rich, modern cities with their towering buildings, eight-lane highways and luxurious shopping centres. （4） On the other hand, there is the poor countryside, where people have retained their traditional lifestyle. （5） A stark contrast can clearly be observed between the cities and the countryside

【点评】

C 最为混乱。它既不按演绎法来写,也不按归纳法来写,所以读者看完后一头雾水,似乎知道作者在说什么,但是又说不清楚作者的论点到底是什么。

我们再做下面的练习,把 a,b,c,d,e 的顺序重新排列,使文章具有一定的逻辑性。

A large number of countries have had difficulty in repaying international debts which they contracted in times when loans were easily available and interest rates were low. In many cases institutions such as the International Monetary Fund have spread repayments over longer periods or arranged further loans. However, in return for these arrangements, the countries concerned have had to accept structural adjustment programmes which have imposed drastic changes on their economic policies. These programmes have usually obliged countries to cut government spending and increase exports in order to earn foreign exchange so that the debts can be repaid.

a. Many farmers now grow flowers, strawberries and similar crops whereas in the past they grew maize and beans.

b. Countries have been forced to switch from their traditional production of food crops for national consumption to the cultivation of crops for export.

c. Food crops such as maize and beans have relatively little earning power as exports.

d. Crops such as flowers and strawberries can be sold to rich consumers in other countries and so have a high potential for earning foreign exchange.

e. In many countries the greatest impact of structural adjustment programmes has been in agriculture.

正确顺序应该是:ebcda 或 ebdca。

e 句属于结论性句子,应该放在段首,即许多国家的经济结构调整主要是对农业结构的调整。b 句是对该结论进行进一步细化,即从消费类农作物的种植调整到出口型农作物的种植。c和d句是分别举例，c说消费类的农作物无出口价值赚不了外汇，d说出口型的农作物可以为国家带来外汇收入。因为c和d是具体的例子，先说c还是先说d对文章结构的影响都不大。a是c和d的结果，所以放在最后说。

第十二节　学会使用关联词

恰当地使用关联词,可以使句子和句子之间的关系更加紧密,为读者的阅读指明一个方向。如关联词使用不当或没有关联词,会使文章的逻辑性大大降低,让读者不知所云。近年在托福考试及其他一些基于计算机的考试项目中,作文阅卷部分已经开始使用电脑阅卷,即用 E-rater 电子作文评分系统。该电子阅卷系统的一个重要原理就是,让电脑寻找一个考生作文中使用的关联词,如果电脑发现一篇作文里缺少关联词,电脑就会认为该考生的逻辑思维欠缺。虽然 SAT 不是基于计算机的考试,但和 GMAT、TOEFL 一样,都是 ETS 命题的考试,所以在我们做 SAT 作文时,一定要注意使用关联词。

文章讲究起承转合,而关联词的使用,可以使这样的起承转合更加清晰。在英文中,经常被使用的关联词可以分类如下:

表示举例：for example, for instance, as an example, as a case, in point, as an illustration, such as, namely, that is, like, say

表示比较：similarly, likewise, in the same way, equally important, like, both, the same as, in common

表示对照：on the contrary, on the other hand, otherwise, unlike, in contrast, whereas, rather than, conversely, instead, by contrast

表示让步：although, nevertheless, however, but, yet, admittedly, it is true ... but, in spite of, even though, granted that

表示原因：because, because of, as, since, for, owing to, due to, on account of, on the ground of, as a result of, result from, thanks to

表示结果：thus, so, consequently, hence, therefore, accordingly, as a result, for this reason, as a consequence, on that account, it follows that, result in

表示强调：chiefly, especially, indeed, in fact, certainly, particularly, to be sure, actually, above all, surely, most important of all, even worse, no doubt, needless to say

表示列举：first, second, in the first place, first of all, to begin with, in the second place, next, also, besides, furthermore, moreover, in addition, what is more, beyond that, for one thing, for another, finally

表示总结：in conclusion, in short, in brief, in summary, on the whole, finally, to sum up, to conclude, in a word

表示开场：generally speaking, comparatively speaking, in general, in a sense, in a way, in my opinion, in some cases, nowadays, recently, currently, obviously, clearly

值得注意的是，在上述常用关联词中，有一些属于连词，也有很多不是连词，所以在使用有关关联词的时候，要注意发生串句错误。比如 therefore、consequently、however 等词，看上去像是连词，但其实都不是，在使用这些关联词时，它们前面必须是句号或分号，否则就犯了不间断句子的错误。

在实际运用中，我们建议同学们多看优秀的范文，多读经典的议论文，看看别人是怎么样使用这些关联词的。

我们来比较下面的两篇文章。两篇文章讲的是同一个内容，但由于 Paragraph A 缺少了关联词，所以整个篇幅显得很混乱，而 Paragraph B 由于关联词使用得当，让读者觉得很清楚（Paragraph B 里的关联词都用黑体字标明）。请大家仔细体会两篇文章给我们带来的不同感受。

Paragraph A

Bilingualism is commonly defined as proficiency in two languages. Bilingual people rarely have an equal level of competence in all aspects of two languages. Many bilinguals are only able to use each of their two languages fluently in specific areas of their daily life. One language may be spoken at home with family and friends and the other at work or in school or college. One language will be restricted to more colloquial uses and may be only rarely if ever used in writing; the other will be used in more formal contexts and writing skills will be necessary. Bilinguals speaking together may shift from one language to the other in the course of a single conversation. Such shifts seem to follow the linguistic needs and feelings of the speakers as they switch from one topic to another. The choice of one language or the other seems to be influenced by the identity of the speakers, the context and the topic of communication.

Paragraph B

Bilingualism is commonly defined as proficiency in two languages. **However,** bilingual people rarely have an equal level of competence in all aspects of two languages. **On the contrary,** many bilinguals are only able to use each of their two languages fluently in specific areas of their daily life. **For example,** one language may be spoken at home with family and friends and the other at work or in school or college. **Consequently,** one language will be restricted to more colloquial uses and may be only rarely if ever used in writing; the other will be used in more formal contexts and writing skills will be necessary. **Moreover,** bilinguals speaking together may switch from one language to the other in the course of a single conversation. Such shifts seem to follow the linguistic needs and feelings of the speakers as they move from one topic to another. In a word, the choice of one language or the other therefore seems to be influenced by the identity of the speakers, the context and the topic of communication.

为使同学们对关联词有更进一步的认识,我们做下面的练习。请从刚刚列举的关联词分类中寻找适当的关联词来完成句子。在做练习之前,建议大家先把文章的大概意思弄明白,了解句子和句子之间的逻辑关系后,再决定选择什么样的关联词。

There is considerable evidence to indicate that the best age to start learning a second language is early childhood. (1)For example the young children of immigrant families seem to learn their new language with apparent ease and soon speak it much more fluently than their parents. (2)What's more some research has shown that immigrants who arrive in their new country of residence before the age of fifteen consistently achieve a high level of competence; (3) However , those who arrive after that age vary considerably in the levels which they eventually reach. (4)Therefore In short , in terms of ultimate levels of achievement, it appears to be preferable to begin learning a second language before the age of fifteen. (5) Nevertheless, while this may be true of immigrants acquiring the language of their new community, it is not necessarily the case for people learning a second language in other circumstances. Immigrants are immersed in the second-language environment and are presumably very highly motivated to succeed in learning the language for reasons of social and economic integration. (6)On contrast children or adults learning a second language outside the country where the language is spoken may only be exposed to it for two or three hours a week at school or college. (7) Also , children in particular may foresee little opportunity for using the language in the future and may (8) thus have little motivation for learning it;

(9) *on the other hand*_____, adults may need to learn the language for a particular purpose and are (10) *consequently*_____ likely to be well motivated. These and other factors may lessen if not nullify the apparent advantage of children over adults. (11) *In conclusion*_____, it is important to take into account the circumstances in which learning takes place when considering the best age to begin learning a second language.

参考答案

1. For example / For instance

2. Moreover / Furthermore / In addition

3. in contrast / however / on the contrary

4. Therefore / Consequently

5. However / Nonetheless / Nevertheless

6. In contrast / However / On the other hand

7. Moreover / Furthermore / In addition

8. therefore / consequently

9. in contrast / however / on the other hand

10. therefore / consequently

11. In conclusion / To sum up

第十三节　句子内容的摆放顺序

写作是为了传达信息,而信息的传达是靠句子完成的。为了有效传达信息,就必须学会对句子内容进行调整,作者要学会使用不同的方法把读者的注意力吸引到他要表达的核心信息上。

一般来说,在一个句子里,对于信息的组织,要遵循这样的原则:**把新信息放到句子的后半部分,而提到过的旧信息要放到句子的前半部分**,这样的句子才会有承上启下的功能。如果把新信息放到句首,给读者有目不暇接的感觉,很容易造成思维上的过分跳跃,从而不能正确理解作者的信息传递。

我们分析下面这篇文章:

(1) Average life expectancy has increased considerably in many parts of the world over the last one hundred years. (2) Improvements in medicine and higher standards of living are the main reasons for this. (3) Yet despite these changes, the maximum human lifespan of about 120 years has not increased. (4) However, delaying the process of growing old may make it possible to extend this limit. (5) Genetic engineering may be one way of slowing down the process. (6) The lifespan of flies has already been doubled in experiments using genetic engineering. (7) Taking additional vitamin E may also help to delay the process. (8) Certain chemicals which can attack the body's cells are neutralised by vitamin E. (9) To sum up, extending the maximum human lifespan may be possible using these two means.

【点评】

第二句的 improvements in medicine and higher standards of living 属于新信息,应该放到句子的后半部分,而 reason for this 中 this 指的是第一句的内容,是旧信息,应放到第二句的前半部分。第三句很好,despite these changes 中的 changes,就是第二句的内容,对第三句来说是旧信息,所以被放到了第三句的前面。

第四句的问题是,this limit 指的是第三句中 120 岁的人类预期寿命,是旧信息,应该放到第四句的前半部分。同样,第五句的 genetic engineering 是新信息,应该放在第五句的后半部分;而对第六句来讲,genetic engineering 就是旧信息了,应该在第六句的前面。第七句的 process 也是属于旧信息,应该在句子的前半部分,而第八句的 vitamin E 是第七句的内容，应该放在第八句的前半部分。对于最后一句，two means 指的是第六、七和八句的两种延长寿命的办法，宜放在最后一句的前面。

综合以上分析，这篇语序混乱的文章经修改后如下，请特别注意黑体处用法的奥妙：

（1）Average life expectancy has increased considerably in many parts of the world over the last one hundred years. （2）**The main reasons for this** are improvements in medicine and higher standards of living. （3）Yet **despite these changes**, there has been no increase in the maximum human lifespan of about 120 years. （4）However, it may be possible to extend this limit by delaying the process of growing old. （5）One way of slowing down the process may be by genetic engineering. （6）**This** has already been used in experiments to double the lifespan of flies. （7）**The process** may also be delayed by taking additional vitamin E. （8）**This** neutralizes certain chemicals which can attack the body's cells. （9）To sum up, these two means may make it possible to extend the maximum human lifespan.

改动后的文章虽然讲的是同一个内容，但由于采用了"旧信息放在句首，新信息放在句尾"的原则，读者在阅读时感觉轻松多了，句子和句子之间的逻辑关系也更清楚了。

请同学们做下面的练习，以进一步了解我们刚才谈到的句子信息组织原则。

Read the following text and choose the sentence in italics (a or b) which you think fits best in each context.

---

1. The process of growing old or ageing involves several changes in the human body. Some of the more obvious external ones are the loss of hair and wrinkles in the skin.

   a. *An increase in blood pressure and the loss of brain cells are examples of internal changes.*

   ⓑ *Examples of internal changes are an increase in blood pressure and the loss of brain cells.*

   ... In addition, ageing also commonly brings a deterioration in the senses of hearing and sight.

2. The passing of time is often considered to be the main cause of the symptoms of ageing in the body. However, this explanation is rather simplistic. In fact, the process of ageing involves several important factors ...

   ⓐ *First, it is influenced by the body's genetic constitution.*

   b. *First, the body's genetic constitution influences it.*

   ... This has been shown by experiments in which scientists have used genetic engineering to increase the lifespan of flies.

3. The ageing process seems to be controlled by a relatively small number of genes ...

   a. *The fact that some types of animals have similar genes but different lifespans demonstrates this.*

   ⓑ *This is demonstrated by the fact that some types of animals have similar genes but different lifespans.*

   ... For example, chimpanzees have about 99% of the same genes as humans but live for less than half as long.

4. Another significant factor in the ageing process is the deterioration of the body caused by certain chemicals called free radicals ...

   a. *When food and oxygen are converted into energy, the body's metabolism produces these chemicals.*

   ⓑ *These chemicals are produced by the body's metabolism when food and oxygen are converted into energy.*

   ... They can destroy proteins and DNA, the acid which carries genetic information in the body's cells.

5. Some protection against the damage caused by free radicals seems to be offered by vitamin E ...

   ⓐ *High levels of it were found by a scientific study in the bodies of people over 100 years old.*

   b. *A scientific study of people over 100 years old found high levels of it in their bodies.*

6. In addition to these two factors, there are many others which can affect the speed at which the body ages. One example is sugar, or glucose to be more precise ...

   a. *Harmful changes to proteins in the body can result from the presence of glucose in the blood.*

   b. *The presence of glucose in the blood can result in harmful changes to proteins in the body.*

   ... These changes can make the body work less efficiently.

7. The problems caused by glucose can be seen in people who suffer from diabetes, a disease in which there is too much sugar in the blood ...

   a. *Stiffness of body joints and heart disease are two common symptoms of this illness.*

   b. *Two common symptoms of this illness are stiffness of body joints and heart disease.*

   ... These problems are often associated with old age.

8. One surprising way in which it may be possible to extend lifespan is by reducing the intake of calories, in other words, by eating less. For example, rats and mice which are given a reduced diet in experiments live 30 to 40 per cent longer than normal ...

   a. *This increase seems to be caused by a change in the way the body's cells use energy.*

   b. *A change in the way the body's cells use energy seems to cause this increase.*

   ... It is possible that reducing the supply of energy to the cells slows down the metabolism.

9. Evidence of this is also provided by an experiment which examined the effect of a reduced diet on a group of monkeys ...

   a. *After several months on a regime in which their food intake was cut by 30 per cent, the monkeys' body temperature fell by 1℃.*

   b. *The monkeys' body temperature fell by 1℃ after several months on a regime in which their food intake was cut by 30 per cent.*

. . . This led scientists to predict that the monkeys could live for as much as 20 per cent longer than normal.

10. A similar phenomenon seems to be demonstrated by an experiment in which people lived in a specially restricted environment. These people's normal food intake was reduced for a period of several months . . .

a. *A number of changes in their bodily functions took place as a result of this reduction: their blood pressure and cholesterol levels fell and the immune systems of their bodies worked more efficiently.*

b. *This reduction resulted in a number of changes in their bodily functions: their blood pressure and cholesterol levels fell and the immune systems of their bodies worked more efficiently.*

. . . These changes indicate that the ageing process is working more slowly and thus that lifespan is likely to be longer.

【参考答案】

1. b 2. a 3. b 4. b 5. a 6. b 7. b 8. a 9. a 10. b

第十四节　主句和从句的使用问题

上一节我们谈到信息摆放的问题，这一节谈的是主句和从句的使用问题。

句子的目的是为了表达信息，信息又分重要信息和次要信息。一个句子包含的信息其实是非常复杂的，一个有经验的写作者应该学会组织信息，让读者看了句子后对其核心信息一目了然。如果没有经验，往往把句子的信息随意摆放，虽然信息都讲到了，但由于缺乏技巧，会使整个句子看上去就是一个大杂烩，让读者不得要领。

在写作中，我们还要遵循的一个原则就是：**重要信息用主句形式表达，次要信息用从句形式表达（或使用各种各样的短语来表达）**。一篇优秀的英文作文，读者哪怕略过所有的从句和短语，仅仅是看主句，也能很清楚这篇文章的主题和内容。

下面是介绍 Arctic(北极地区)的文章，三篇文章的信息含量是一样的，但主句和从句的使用方式不同，导致这三篇文章的质量大不一样。

Paragraph A

(1) The Arctic is the northernmost region on Earth. (2) It is centred on the North Pole. (3) It comprises all of the area located north of the latitude 66° North. (4) This line marks the Arctic Circle. (5) The Arctic includes most of Greenland. (6) This is the largest island in the world. (7) The region also includes the Arctic Ocean. (8) This is the world's smallest ocean. (9) It covers an area of almost 14 million square kilometres.

【点评】

这个文章的所有句子都是主句，都是简单句，导致整篇文章缺乏重点，没有核心，给人感觉就是信息大杂烩。

Paragraph B

(1) The Arctic, which is the northernmost region on Earth, is centred on the North Pole. (2) The latitude 66° North, which is the southern limit of the area, marks the Arctic Circle. (3) Greenland, most of which lies inside the Arctic, is the largest island in the world. (4) The Arctic Ocean, which is also included in the region, is the world's smallest ocean, covering an area of about 14 million square

kilometres.

【点评】

这篇文章虽然使用了主句和从句,但使用不当。既然是介绍 Arctic 的文章,所有关于 Arctic 的句子应该作为主句摆放,但原文并没有这样。比如第二句核心信息是 the latitude 66° North,第三句的核心信息变成了 Greenland。

Paragraph C

(1) The Arctic is the northernmost region on Earth. (2) Centred on the North Pole, it comprises all of the area located north of the latitude 66° North, which marks the Arctic Circle. (3) The Arctic includes most of Greenland, which is the largest island in the world. (4) The region also includes the Arctic Ocean, which is the world's smallest ocean, covering an area of about 14 million square kilometres.

【点评】

这是三篇文章中把主句和从句处理得最好的。第一句谈 Arctic 的独特位置;第二句介绍它的大概范围;第三句进一步谈到 Arctic 包括 Greenland,并把 Greenland 的信息作为从句形式处理;第四句的信息处理方式同第三句。全篇让人感觉到重点就是 Arctic,它的位置和它包括的领域都用从句的形式表达出来,使得整个文章重点突出,主次分明。

我们看下面介绍 Antarctica 的两篇文章。其中 B 把主从句处理得非常恰当,而 A 对主从句的处理就不是那么妥当了,从而使作者的信息传达不是那么有效。请同学们用心体会两篇文章的差异,进一步理解"重要信息用主句表达,次要信息用从句表达"这一基本原则。

The Structure of Antarctica

Paragraph A

(1) Antarctica is the fifth largest continent in the world. (2) It has a total land area of 14,245,000 square kilometres. (3) The continent, which extends from the South Pole roughly to the Antarctic Circle, is divided into East and West Antarctica. (4) The Antarctic ice cap, which joins these two areas, is up to 4,000 metres thick and covers 98% of the continent. (5) East Antarctica, which is a vast semi-circular area, is the larger of the two regions. (6) West Antarctica, on the other hand, is more irregular in shape. (7) The Weddell Sea and the Ross Sea,

which cut deeply into this region from opposite sides, are named after nineteenth century explorers. (8) The only part of West Antarctica to cross the Antarctic Circle is the Antarctic Peninsula. (9) This part, which is the mildest and most accessible part of the whole continent, stretches north towards the southern tip of South America. (10) Consequently, the peninsula has the greatest concentration of scientific research stations on the continent.

Paragraph B

(1) Antarctica is the fifth largest continent in the world. (2) It has a total land area of 14,245,000 square kilometres. (3) The continent, which extends from the South Pole roughly to the Antarctic Circle, is divided into East and West Antarctica. (4) *These two areas are joined by the Antarctic ice cap, which is up to 4,000 metres thick and covers 98% of the continent.* (5) *East Antarctica, which is the larger of the two regions, is a vast semi-circular area.* (6) West Antarctica, on the other hand, is more irregular in shape. (7) *The Weddell Sea and the Ross Sea, which are named after nineteenth century explorers, cut deeply into this region from opposite sides.* (8) The only part of West Antarctica to cross the Antarctic Circle is the Antarctic Peninsula. (9) *This part, which stretches north towards the southern tip of South America, is the mildest and most accessible part of the whole continent.* (10) Consequently, the peninsula has the greatest concentration of scientific research stations on the continent.

请根据我们刚才谈到的主从句原则做下面的练习：

> Read the following text carefully and then choose the sentence in italics (a or b) which you think fits best in each context.

1. Greenland, or Kalaallit Nunaat as it is officially known, is the largest island in the world.

　　a. *It has a land area of about 2,175,600 square kilometres, four-fifths of which are covered with ice.*

　　b. *Ice covers over four-fifths of its land area, which measures 2,175,600 square kilometres.*

2. In terms of its position on the Earth's surface, it stretches between 60° and 84° North, and between 20° and 60° West.

   a. *Most of the country lies within the Arctic, which extends from about 66° North to the North Pole.*

   b. *The Arctic, which encompasses most of the country, extends from about 66° North to the North Pole.*

3. To the north of Greenland is the Arctic Ocean.

   a. *This ocean, which extends from the northern coast of Greenland as far as Siberia, is mostly covered with a thick ice pack throughout the year*

   b. *This ocean, which is mostly covered with a thick ice pack throughout the year, extends from the northern coast of Greenland as far as Siberia.*

4. It is more or less centred on the North Pole.

   a. *To the east of Greenland lies Iceland, which is another, much smaller island.*

   b. *Iceland, which lies to the east of Greenland, is another, much smaller island.*

5. a. *The Denmark Strait, which separates these two countries, is the channel of water to the south-east.*

   b. *These two countries are separated by the Denmark Strait, which is the channel of water to the south-east.*

6. South of Greenland are the vast waters of the Atlantic Ocean.

   a. *Finally, Canada, which is separated from Greenland by the Davis Strait, is situated to the west.*

   b. *Finally, Canada, which is situated to the west, is separated from Greenland by the Davis Strait.*

7. The south-west coast is where the majority of the population live.

   a. *This coastline is warmed by the North Atlantic Drift, which is a current of warm water in the North Atlantic Ocean.*

b. *The North Atlantic Drift, which warms this coastline, is a current of warm water in the North Atlantic Ocean.*

8. The climate on this coast is therefore more hospitable than the extreme conditions in other parts of the country.

a. *The capital, which is situated on this coast, is called Nuuk*

b. *The capital, which is called Nuuk, is situated on this coast.*

9. a. *The Eskimo or Inuit, who are thought to have first appeared in Greenland in the thirteenth century, are native inhabitants of a large area stretching halfway around the Arctic Circle.*

b. *The Eskimo or Inuit, who are native inhabitants of a large area stretching halfway around the Arctic Circle, are thought to have first appeared in Greenland in the thirteenth century.*

10. Norse settlers had already reached Greenland from Scandinavia in the tenth century, but they later underwent a period of decline.

a. *British explorers Frobisher and Davis, who reached the island in the sixteenth century, found that the Norse colonists had died out or been assimilated with the Eskimo population.*

b. *British explorers Frobisher and Davis, who found that the Norse colonists had died out or been assimilated with the Eskimo population, reached the island in the sixteenth century.*

However, the country was eventually re-colonised by Norway early in the eighteenth century and became a Danish colony in 1815. In 1979 Greenland was granted home rule

【参考答案】

1. a　2. a　3. b　4. a　5. b　6. a　7. a　8. b　9. b　10. a

第五章　SAT 历届真题作文

　　本章收集了 SAT 自 2006 年 1 月到 2009 年 3 月的真题作文。从中不难看出，SAT 的作文题出来出去，就是一些老生常谈的题目。建议同学们在时间充裕的情况下，最好能把这几十道作文题认真写一遍。2006 年的题目可以按一篇作文 35 分钟的时间来写；写了十几篇后，2007 年的作文题要把时间限定在 30 分钟内来写；而 2008 年和 2009 年的作文题就要严格限定在 25 分钟内完成。这样可以不断地提高写作速度，逐步达到在 25 分钟内完成一篇作文的要求。

　　这些作文题的写作模式，可以参考本书介绍的方式。作文写出来后，不妨请自己身边的英文高手或学校的老师帮忙修改，一方面看内容是否合适，另外一方面不断地纠正自己的语法错误，提高自己遣词造句的能力。

　　对于一些比较棘手的作文题，建议大家在网上寻找相关素材，并将这些素材分类整理，熟记于心，因为这些素材很有可能就会在考试的时候派上用场。

　　英文中有句老生常谈的话是 Practice makes perfect，虽然简单，却有深刻的道理！

2006 年 1 月真题作文题

Prompt 1

Think carefully about the issue presented in the following excerpt and the assignment below.

> Every important discovery results from patience, perseverance, and concentration — sometimes continuing for months or years — on one specific subject. A person who wants to discover a new truth must remain absorbed by that one subject, must pay no attention to any thought that is unrelated to the problem.
>
> Adapted from Santiago Ramon Cajal, *Advice for a Young Investigator*

Assignment: Are all important discoveries the result of focusing on one subject? Plan and write an essay in which you develop your point of view on this issue. Support your position with reasoning and examples taken from your reading, studies, experience, or observations.

Prompt 2

Think carefully about the issue presented in the following excerpt and the assignment below.

> A colleague of the great scientist James Watson remarked that Watson was always " lounging around, arguing about problems instead of doing experiments. " He concluded that "There is more than one way of doing good science. " It was Watson's form of idleness, the scientist went on to say , that allowed him to slove "the greatest of all biological problems: the discovery of the structure of DNA". It is a point worth remembering in a society overly concerned with efficiency.
>
> Adapted from John C. Polanyi, *Understanding Discovery*

Assignment: Do people accomplish more when they are allowed to do things in their own way? Plan and write an essay in which you develop your point of view on this issue. Support your position with reasoning and examples taken from your reading, studies, experience, or observations.

Prompt 3

Think carefully about the issue presented in the following excerpt and the assignment below.

> I do not feel terrible about my mistakes, though I grieve the pain they have sometimes caused others. Our lives are "experiments with truth", and in experiment negative results are at least as important as successes. I have no idea how I would have learned the truth about myself and my calling without the mistakes I have made.
>
> Adapted from Parker Palmer, *Let Your Life Speak*

Assignment: Is it necessary to make mistakes, even when doing so has negative consequences for other people? Plan and write an essay in which you develop your point of view on this issue. Support your position with reasoning and examples taken from your reading, studies, experience, or observations.

Prompt 4

Think carefully about the issue presented in the following excerpt and the assignment below.

> An actor, when his cue came, was unable to move onto the stage. He said, "I can't get in, the chair is in the way." And the producer said, "Use the difficulty. If it's a drama, pick the chair up and smash it. If it's a comedy fall over it." From this experience the actor concluded that in any situation in life that is negative, there is something positive you can do with it.
>
> Adapted from Lawrence Eisenberg, *Caine Scrutiny*

Assignment: Can any obstacle or disadvantage be turned into something good? Plan and write an essay in which you develop your point of view on this issue. Support your position with reasoning and examples taken from your reading, studies, experience, or observations.

2006 年 5 月真题作文题

Prompt 1

Think carefully about the issue presented in the following excerpt and the assignment below.

Some people claim that each individual is solely responsible for what happens to him or her. But the claim that we ought to take absolute responsibility for the kinds of people we are and the kinds of lives we lead suggests that we have complete control over our lives. We do not. The circumstances of our lives can make it more or less impossible to make certain kinds of choices.

Adapted from Gordon D. Marino, *I Think You Should Be Responsible; Me, I'm Not So Sure*

Assignment: Are we free to make our own decisions or are we limited in the choices we can make? Plan and write an essay in which you develop your point of view on this issue. Support your position with reasoning and examples taken from your reading, studies, experience, or observations.

Prompt 2

Think carefully about the issue presented in the following excerpt and the assignment below.

Certainly anyone who insists on condemning all lies should think about what would happen if we could reliably tell when our family, friends, colleagues, and government leaders were deceiving us. It is tempting to think that the world would become a better place without the deceptions that seem to interfere with our attempts are genuine communication. On the other hand, perhaps there is such a thing as too much honesty.

Adapted from Allison Kornet, *The Truth About Lying*

Assignment: Would the world be a better place if everyone always told the complete truth? Plan and write an essay in which you develop your point of view on this issue. Support your position with reasoning and examples taken from your reading, studies, experience, or observations.

Prompt 3

Think carefully about the issue presented in the following excerpt and the assignment below.

> It is not that people dislike being part of a community; it is just that they care about their individual freedoms more. People value neighborliness and social interaction until being part of a group requires them to limit their freedom for the larger good of the group. But a community or group cannot function effectively unless people are willing to se aside their personal interests.
>
> Adapted from Warren Johnson, *The Future Is Not What It Used To Be*

Assignment: Does the success of a community — whether it is a class, a team, a family, a nation, or any other group — depend upon people's willingness to limit their personal interests? Plan and write an essay in which you develop your point of view on this issue. Support your position with reasoning and examples taken from your reading, studies, experience, or observations.

Prompt 4

Think carefully about the issue presented in the following excerpt and the assignment below.

> There is an old saying: "A person with one watch knows what time it is; a person with two watches isn't so sure." In other words, a person who looks at an object or event from two different angles sees something different from each position. Moreover, two or more people looking at the same thing may each perceive something different. In other words, truth, like beauty, may lie in the eye of the beholder.
>
> Adapted from Gregory D. Foster, *Ethics: Time to Revisit the Basics*

Assignment：Does the truth change depending on how people look at things? Plan and write an essay in which you develop your point of view on this issue. Support your position with reasoning and examples taken from your reading, studies, experience, or observations.

2006 年 10 月真题作文题

Prompt 1

Think carefully about the issue presented in the following excerpt and the assignment below.

> While some people promote competition as the only way to achieve success, others emphasize the power of cooperation. Intense rivalry at work or play or engaging in competition involving ideas or skills may indeed drive people either to avoid failure or to achieve important victories.
>
> In a complex world, however, cooperation is much more likely to produce significant, lasting accomplishments.

Assignment: Do people achieve more success by cooperation than by competition? Plan and write an essay in which you develop your point of view on this issue. Support your position with reasoning and examples taken from your reading, studies, experience, or observations.

Prompt 2

Think carefully about the issue presented in the following excerpt and the assignment below.

> Sometimes it is necessary to challenge what people in authority claim to be true. Although some respect for authority is, no doubt, necessary in order for any group or organization to function, questioning the people in charge-even if they are experts or leaders in their fields-makes us better thinkers. It forces all concerned to defend old ideas and decisions and to consider new ones. Sometimes it can even correct old errors in thought and put an end to wrong actions.

Assignment: Is it important to question the ideas and decisions of people in positions of authority? Plan and write an essay in which you develop your point of view on this issue. Support your position with reasoning and examples taken from your reading, studies, experience, or observations.

Prompt 3

Think carefully about the issue presented in the following excerpt and the assignment below.

> We don't really learn anything properly until there is a problem, until we make a mistake, until something fails to go as we had hoped. When everything is working well, with no problems or failures, what incentive do we have to try something new? We are only motivated to learn when we experience difficulties.
>
> Adapted from Alain de Botton, *How Proust Can Change Your Life: Not a Novel*

Assignment: Does true learning only occur when we experience difficulties? Plan and write an essay in which you develop your point of view on this issue. Support your position with reasoning and examples taken from your reading, studies, experience, or observations.

Prompt 4

Think carefully about the issue presented in the following excerpt and the assignment below.

> There are two kinds of pretending. There is the bad kind, as when a person falsely promises to be your friends. But there is also a good kind, where the pretense eventually turns into the real thing. For example, when you are not feeling particularly friendly, the best thing you can do, very often, is to act in a friendly manner. In a few minutes, you may really be feeling friendlier.
>
> Adapted from a book by C. S. Lewis

Assignment: Can deception-pretending that something is true when it is not-sometimes have good results? Plan and write an essay in which you develop your point of view on this issue. Support your position with reasoning and examples taken from your reading, studies, experience, or observations.

2006 年 11 月真题作文题

Prompt 1

Think carefully about the issue presented in the following excerpt and the assignment below.

> It is wrong to think of ourselves as indispensable. We would love to think that our contributions are essential, but we are mistaken if we think that any one person has made the world what it is today. The contributions of individual people are seldom as important or as necessary as we think they are.

Assignment: Do we put too much value on the ideas or actions of individual people? Plan and write an essay in which you develop your point of view on this issue. Support your position with reasoning and examples taken from your reading, studies, experience, or observations.

Prompt 2

Think carefully about the issue presented in the following excerpt and the assignment below.

> Many people deny that stories about characters and events that are not real can teach us about ourselves or about the world around us. They claim that literature does not offer us worthwhile information about the real world. These people argue that the feelings and ideas we gain from books and stories obstruct, rather than contribute to, clear thought.
>
> Adapted from Jennifer L. McMahon, *The Function of Fiction*

Assignment: Can books and stories about characters and events that are not real teach us anything useful? Plan and write an essay in which you develop your point of view on this issue. Support your position with reasoning and examples taken from your reading, studies, experience, or observations.

Prompt 3

Think carefully about the issue presented in the following excerpt and the assignment below.

> "No one is perfect." There are few among us who would disagree with this familiar statement. Certain that perfection is an impossible goal, many people willingly accept flaws and shortcomings in themselves and others. Yet such behavior leads to failure. People can only succeed if they try to achieve perfection in everything they do.

Assignment: Can people achieve success only if they aim to be perfect? Plan and write an essay in which you develop your point of view on this issue. Support your position with reasoning and examples taken from your reading, studies, experience, or observations.

Prompt 4

Think carefully about the issue presented in the following excerpt and the assignment below.

> Everybody has some choice. People are always blaming their circumstances for what they are. I don't believe in circumstances. The people who get on in this world are the people who get up and look for the circumstances they want and, if they can't find them, make them.
>
> Adapted from George Bernard Shaw, *Mrs. Warren's Profession*

Assignment: Do success and happiness depend on the choices people make rather than on factors beyond their control? Plan and write an essay in which you develop your point of view on this issue. Support your position with reasoning and examples taken from your reading, studies, experience, or observations.

2006 年 12 月真题作文题

Prompt 1

Think carefully about the issue presented in the following excerpt and the assignment below.

> In order to be the most productive and successful people that we are capable of being, we must be willing to ignore the opinions of others. It is only when we are completely indifferent to others' opinions of us-when we are not concerned about how others think of us-that we can achieve our most important goals.

Assignment: Are people more likely to be productive and successful when they ignore the opinions of others? Plan and write an essay in which you develop your point of view on this issue. Support your position with reasoning and examples taken from your reading, studies, experience, or observations.

Prompt 2

Think carefully about the issue presented in the following excerpt and the assignment below.

> In many circumstances, optimism — the expectation that one's ideas and plans will always turn out for the best — is unwarranted. In these situations what is needed is not an upbeat view but a realistic one. There are times when people need to take a tough-minded view of the possibilities of success, give up, and invest their energies elsewhere rather than find reasons to continue to pursue the original project or idea.
>
> Adapted from Martin E. P. Seligman, *Learned Optimism*

Assignment: Is it better for people to be realistic or optimistic? Plan and write an essay in which you develop your point of view on this issue. Support your position with reasoning and examples taken from your reading, studies, experience, or observations.

Prompt 3

Think carefully about the issue presented in the following excerpt and the assignment below.

> It is easy to make judgments about people and their actions when we do not know anything about their circumstances or what motivated them to take those actions. But we should look beyond a person's actions. When people do things that we consider outrageous, inconsiderate, or harmful, we should try to understand why they acted as they did.

Assignment: Is it important to try to understand people's motivations before judging their actions? Plan and write an essay in which you develop your point of view on this issue. Support your position with reasoning and examples taken from your reading, studies, experience, or observations.

Prompt 4

Think carefully about the issue presented in the following excerpt and the assignment below.

> Abraham Lincoln said, "Most people are about as happy as they make up their minds to be." In other words, our personal level of satisfaction is entirely within our control. Otherwise, why would the same experience disappoint one person but delight another? Happiness is not an accident but a choice.

Assignment: Is happiness something over which people have no control, or can people choose to be happy? Plan and write an essay in which you develop your point of view on this issue. Support your position with reasoning and examples taken from your reading, studies, experience, or observations.

2007 年 1 月真题作文题

Prompt 1

Think carefully about the issue presented in the following excerpt and the assignment below.

> Many people believe that our government should do more to solve our problems. After all, how can one individual create more jobs or make roads safer or improve the schools or help to provide any of the other benefits that we have come to enjoy? And yet expecting that the government — rather than individuals — should always come up with the solutions to society's ills may have made us less self-reliant, undermining our independence and self-sufficiency.

Assignment: Should people take more responsibility for solving problems that affect their communities or the nation in general? Plan and write an essay in which you develop your point of view on this issue. Support your position with reasoning and examples taken from your reading, studies, experience, or observations.

Prompt 2

Think carefully about the issue presented in the following excerpt and the assignment below.

> Most human beings spend their lives doing work they hate and work that the world does not need. It is of prime importance that you learn early what you want to do and whether or not the world needs this service. The return from your work must be the satisfaction that work brings you and the world's need of that work. Income is not money, it is satisfaction; it is creation; it is beauty.
>
> Adapted from W. E. B. Du Bois, *The Autobiography of W. E. B. Du Bois: A Soliloquy on Viewing My Life from the Last Decade of Its First Century*

Assignment: Is it more important to do work that one finds fulfilling or work that pays well? Plan and write an essay in which you develop your point of view on this issue. Support your position with reasoning and examples taken from your reading, studies, experience, or observations.

Prompt 3

Think carefully about the issue presented in the following excerpt and the assignment below.

> The education people receive does not occur primarily in school. Young people are formed by their experiences with parents, teachers, peers, and even strangers on the street, and by the sports teams they play for, the shopping malls they frequent, the songs they hear, and the shows they watch. Schools, while certainly important, constitute only a relatively small part of education.
>
> Adapted from Mihaly Csikszentmihalyi, *Education for the Twenty-First Century*

Assignment: Is education primarily the result of influences other than school? Plan and write an essay in which you develop your point of view on this issue. Support your position with reasoning and examples taken from your reading, studies, experience, or observations.

Prompt 4

Think carefully about the issue presented in the following excerpt and the assignment below.

> If we are dissatisfied with our circumstances, we think about changing them. But the most important and effective changes-in our attitude-hardly occur to us. In other words, we should worry not about how to alter the world around us for the better but about how to change ourselves in order to fit into that world.
>
> Adapted from Michael Hymers, *Wittgenstein*, *Pessimism and Politics*

Assignment: Is it better to change one's attitude than to change one's circumstances?

Plan and write an essay in which you develop your point of view on this issue. Support your position with reasoning and examples taken from your reading, studies, experience, or observations.

2007 年 3 月真题作文题

Prompt 1

Think carefully about the issue presented in the following excerpt and the assignment below.

> · From the time people are very young, they are urged to get along with others, to try to "fit in." Indeed, people are often rewarded for being agreeable and obedient. But this approach is misguided because it promotes uniformity instead of encouraging people to be unique and different. Differences among people give each of us greater perspective and allow us to make better judgments.

Assignment: Is it more valuable for people to fit in than to be unique and different? Plan and write an essay in which you develop your point of view on this issue. Support your position with reasoning and examples taken from your reading, studies, experience, or observations.

Prompt 2

Think carefully about the issue presented in the following excerpt and the assignment below.

> It is easy to imagine that events and experiences in our lives will be perfect, but no matter how good something turns out to be, it can never live up to our expectations. Reality never matches our imaginations. For that reason, we should make sure our plans and goals are modest and attainable. We are much better off when reality surpasses our expectations and something turns out better than we thought it would.
>
> Adapted from Baltasar Gracián y Morales, *The Art of Worldly Wisdom*

Assignment: Is it best to have low expectations and to set goals we are sure of achieving? Plan and write an essay in which you develop your point of view on this issue. Support your position with reasoning and examples taken from your reading, studies, experience, or observations.

Prompt 3

Think carefully about the issue presented in the following excerpt and the assignment below.

> Every event has consequences that are potentially beneficial. We may not always be happy about an experience, but we should at least gain in some way from it. For example, the worldwide gasoline shortage in the early 1970's created many hardships but inspired efforts to conserve energy. Whether the gains are large or small, there is something positive or useful for us in everything that happens to us.

Assignment: Do we really benefit from every event or experience in some way? Plan and write an essay in which you develop your point of view on this issue. Support your position with reasoning and examples taken from your reading, studies, experience, or observations.

2007 年 5 月真题作文题

Prompt 1

Think carefully about the issue presented in the following excerpt and the assignment below.

Materialism: it's the thing that everybody loves to hate. Few aspects of modern life have been more criticized than materialism. But let's face it: materialism — acquiring possessions and spending money — is a vital source of meaning and happiness in our time. People may criticize modern society for being too materialistic, but the fact remains that most of us spend most of our energy producing and consuming more and more stuff.

Adapted from James Twitchell, *Two Cheers for Materialism*

Assignment: Should modern society be criticized for being materialistic? Plan and write an essay in which you develop your point of view on this issue. Support your position with reasoning and examples taken from your reading, studies, experience, or observations.

Prompt 2

Think carefully about the issue presented in the following excerpt and the assignment below.

Knowledge is power. In agriculture, medicine, and industry, for example, knowledge has liberated us from hunger, disease, and tedious labor. Today, however, our knowledge has become so powerful that it is beyond our control. We know how to do many things, but we do not know where, when, or even whether this know-how should be used.

Assignment: Can knowledge be a burden rather than a benefit? Plan and write an essay in which you develop your point of view on this issue. Support your position with reasoning and examples taken from your reading, studies, experience, or observations.

Prompt 3

Think carefully about the issue presented in the following excerpt and the assignment below.

> We do not take the time to determine right from wrong. Reflecting on the difference between right and wrong is hard work. It is so much easier to follow the crowd, going along with what is popular rather than risking the disapproval of others by voicing an objection of any kind.
>
> Adapted from Stephen J. Carter, *Integrity*

Assignment: Is it always best to determine one's own views of right and wrong, or can we benefit from following the crowd? Plan and write an essay in which you develop your point of view on this issue. Support your position with reasoning and examples taken from your reading, studies, experience, or observations.

Prompt 4

Think carefully about the issue presented in the following excerpt and the assignment below.

> It is often the case that revealing the complete truth may bring trouble — discomfort, embarrassment, sadness, or even harm — to oneself or to another person. In these circumstances, it is better not to express our real thoughts and feelings. Whether or not we should tell the truth, therefore, depends on the circumstances.

Assignment: Do circumstances determine whether or not we should tell the truth? Plan and write an essay in which you develop your point of view on this issue. Support your position with reasoning and examples taken from your reading, studies, experience, or observations.

2007 年 6 月真题作文题

Prompt 1

Think carefully about the issue presented in the following excerpt and the assignment below.

> People are happy only when they have their minds fixed on some goal other than their own happiness. Happiness comes when people focus instead on the happiness of others, on the improvement of humanity, on some course of action that is followed not as a means to anything else but as an end in itself. Aiming at something other than their own happiness, they find happiness along the way. The only way to be happy is to pursue some goal external to your own happiness.
>
> Adapted from John Stuart Mill, *Autobiography*

Assignment: Are people more likely to be happy if they focus on goals other than their own happiness? Plan and write an essay in which you develop your point of view on this issue. Support your position with reasoning and examples taken from your reading, studies, experience, or observations.

Prompt 2

Think carefully about the issue presented in the following excerpt and the assignment below.

> Heroes may seem old-fashioned today. Many people are cynical and seem to enjoy discrediting role models more than creating new ones or cherishing those they already have. Some people, moreover, object to the very idea of heroes, arguing that we should not exalt individuals who, after all, are only flesh and blood, just like the rest of us. But we desperately need heroes-to teach us, to captivate us through their words and deeds, to inspire us to greatness.
>
> Adapted from Psychology Today, *How To Be Great*! *What Does It Take To Be A Hero*?

Assignment: Is there a value in celebrating certain individuals as heroes? Plan and write an essay in which you develop your point of view on this issue. Support your position with reasoning and examples taken from your reading, studies, experience, or observations.

Prompt 3

Think carefully about the issue presented in the following excerpt and the assignment below.

> The advancements that have been made over the past hundred years or more are too numerous to count. But has there been progress? Some people would say that the vast number of advancements tells us we have made progress. Others, however, disagree, saying that more is not necessarily better and that real progress — in politics, literature, the arts, science and technology, or any other field — can be achieved only when an advancement truly improves the quality of our lives.

Assignment: Have modern advancements truly improved the quality of people's lives? Plan and write an essay in which you develop your point of view on this issue. Support your position with reasoning and examples taken from your reading, studies, experience, or observations.

Prompt 4

Think carefully about the issue presented in the following excerpt and the assignment below.

> It is not true that prosperity is better for people than adversity. When people are thriving and content, they seldom feel the need to look for ways to improve themselves or their situation. Hardship, on the other hand, forces people to closely examine—and possibly change—their own lives and even the lives of others. Misfortune rather than prosperity helps people to gain a greater understanding of themselves and the world around them.

Assignment: Do people truly benefit from hardship and misfortune? Plan and write an essay in which you develop your point of view on this issue. Support your position with reasoning and examples taken from your reading, studies, experience, or observations.

2007 年 10 月真题作文题

Prompt 1

Think carefully about the issue presented in the following excerpt and the assignment below.

> A person does not simply "receive" his or her identity. Identity is much more than the name or features one is born with. True identity is something people must create for themselves by making choices that are significant and that require a courageous commitment in the face of challenges. Identity means having ideas and values that one lives by.
>
> Adapted from Thomas Merton, *Contemplation in a World of Action*

Assignment: Is identity something people are born with or given, or is it something people create for themselves? Plan and write an essay in which you develop your point of view on this issue. Support your position with reasoning and examples taken from your reading, studies, experience, or observations.

Prompt 2

Think carefully about the issue presented in the following excerpt and the assignment below.

> We value uniqueness and originality, but it seems that everywhere we turn, we are surrounded by ideas and things that are copies or even copies of copies. Writers, artists, and musicians seek new ideas for paintings, books, songs, and movies, but many sadly realize, "It's been done." The same is true for scientists, scholars, and businesspeople. Everyone wants to create something new, but at best we can hope only to repeat or imitate what has already been done.

Assignment: Can people ever be truly original? Plan and write an essay in which you develop your point of view on this issue. Support your position with reasoning and examples taken from your reading, studies, experience, or observations.

Prompt 3

Think carefully about the issue presented in the following excerpt and the assignment below.

> All people who have achieved greatness in something knew what they excelled at. These people identified the skills that made them special — good judgment, or courage, or a special artistic or literary talent — and focused on developing these skills. Yet most people achieve superiority in nothing because they fail to identify and develop their greatest attribute.
>
> Adapted from Baltasar Gracián y Morales, *The Art of Worldly Wisdom*

Assignment: Do people achieve greatness only by finding out what they are especially good at and developing that attribute above all else? Plan and write an essay in which you develop your point of view on this issue. Support your position with reasoning and examples taken from your reading, studies, experience, or observations.

Prompt 4

Think carefully about the issue presented in the following excerpt and the assignment below.

> Having many admirers is one way to become a celebrity, but it is not the way to become a hero. Heroes are self-made. Yet in our daily lives we see no difference between "celebrities" and "heroes." For this reason, we deprive ourselves of real role models. We should admire heroes — people who are famous because they are great-but not celebrities — people who simply seem great because they are famous.
>
> Adapted from Daniel Boorstin, *The Image: A Guide to Pseudo-Events in America*

Assignment：Should we admire heroes but not celebrities? Plan and write an essay in which you develop your point of view on this issue. Support your position with reasoning and examples taken from your reading, studies, experience, or observations.

2007 年 11 月真题作文题

Prompt 1

Think carefully about the issue presented in the following excerpt and the assignment below.

> People today have so many choices. For instance, thirty years ago most television viewers could choose from only a few channels; today there are more than a hundred channels available. And choices do not just abound when it comes to the media. People have more options in almost every area of life. With so much to choose from, how can we not be happy?

Assignment: Does having a large number of options to choose from make people happy? Plan and write an essay in which you develop your point of view on this issue. Support your position with reasoning and examples taken from your reading, studies, experience, or observations.

Prompt 2

Think carefully about the issue presented in the following excerpt and the assignment below.

> We are often urged to solve problems by ignoring traditional approaches and by finding solutions that are innovative or unconventional. We are encouraged to be creative and to trust that a new way of thinking will yield new insights. But innovation may be impractical and unnecessary. The best ways of fixing problems are often the tried-and-true ways.

Assignment: Is it always necessary to find new solutions to problems? Plan and write an essay in which you develop your point of view on this issue. Support your position with reasoning and examples taken from your reading, studies, experience, or observations.

Prompt 3

Think carefully about the issue presented in the following excerpt and the assignment below.

> Many people consider the arts-literature, music, painting, and other creative activities-unnecessary because they provide us with nothing more than entertainment. Yet the arts are extremely valuable because they have much to teach us about the world around us and also because they help people find meaning in life.

Assignment: Is the main value of the arts to teach us about the world around us? Plan and write an essay in which you develop your point of view on this issue. Support your position with reasoning and examples taken from your reading, studies, experience, or observations.

Prompt 4

Think carefully about the issue presented in the following excerpt and the assignment below.

> All people judge or criticize the ideas and actions of others. At times, these criticisms hurt or embarrass the people receiving them. Other criticisms seem to be intended to make the critics appear superior. And yet criticism is essential to our success as individuals and as a society.
>
> Adapted from Ken Petress, *Constructive Criticism: A Tool for Improvement*

Assignment: Is criticism-judging or finding fault with the ideas and actions of others-essential for personal well-being and social progress? Plan and write an essay in which you develop your point of view on this issue. Support your position with reasoning and examples taken from your reading, studies, experience, or observations.

2007 年 12 月真题作文题

Prompt 1

Think carefully about the issue presented in the following excerpt and the assignment below.

> The first problem for all of us is not to learn but to unlearn. We hold on to ideas that were accepted in the past, and we are afraid to give them up. Preconceptions about what is right or wrong, true or false, good or bad are embedded so deeply in our thinking that we honestly may not know that they are there. Whether it's women's role in society or the role of our country in the world, the old assumptions just don't work anymore.
>
> Adapted from Gloria Steinem, *A New Egalitarian Lifestyle*

Assignment: Do people need to "unlearn," or reject, many of their assumptions and ideas? Plan and write an essay in which you develop your point of view on this issue. Support your position with reasoning and examples taken from your reading, studies, experience, or observations.

Prompt 2

Think carefully about the issue presented in the following excerpt and the assignment below.

> Our determination to pursue truth by setting up a fight between two sides leads us to believe that every issue has two sides — no more, no less. If we know both sides of an issue, all of the relevant information will emerge, and the best case will be made for each side. But this process does not always lead to the truth. Often the truth is somewhere in the complex middle, not the oversimplified extremes.
>
> Adapted from Deborah Tannen, *The Argument Culture*

Assignment: Should people choose one of two opposing sides of an issue, or is the truth usually found "in the middle"? Plan and write an essay in which you develop your point of view on this issue. Support your position with reasoning and examples taken from your reading, studies, experience, or observations.

Prompt 3

Think carefully about the issue presented in the following excerpt and the assignment below.

> All around us appearances are mistaken for reality. Clever advertisements create favorable impressions but say little or nothing about the products they promote. In stores, colorful packages are often better than their contents. In the media, how certain entertainers, politicians, and other public figures appear is more important than their abilities. All too often, what we think we see becomes far more important than what really is.

Assignment: Do images and impressions have too much of an effect on people? Plan and write an essay in which you develop your point of view on this issue. Support your position with reasoning and examples taken from your reading, studies, experience, or observations.

Prompt 4

Think carefully about the issue presented in the following excerpt and the assignment below.

> Until fairly recently, technological innovations and inventions were intended to serve basic human needs or desires. Today, however, the most important and urgent problem confronting us is no longer the satisfaction of basic needs. The primary purpose of modern technology is to solve the unintended problems caused by the technology of years past.
>
> Adapted from Dennis Gabor, *Innovations: Scientific, Technological, and Social*

Assignment: Is the most important purpose of technology today different from what it was in the past? Plan and write an essay in which you develop your point of view on this issue. Support your position with reasoning and examples taken from your reading, studies, experience, or observations.

2008 年 1 月真题作文题

Prompt 1

Think carefully about the issue presented in the following excerpt and the assignment below.

> It is better to try to be original than to merely imitate others. People should always try to say, write, think, or create something new. There is little value in merely repeating what has been done before. People who merely copy or use the ideas and inventions of others, no matter how successful they may be, have never achieved anything significant.

Assignment: Is it always better to be original than to imitate or use the ideas of others? Plan and write an essay in which you develop your point of view on this issue. Support your position with reasoning and examples taken from your reading, studies, experience, or observations.

Prompt 2

Think carefully about the issue presented in the following excerpt and the assignment below.

> Often we see people who persist in trying to achieve a particular goal, even when all the evidence indicates that they will be unlikely to achieve it. When they succeed, we consider them courageous for having overcome impossible obstacles. But when they fail, we think of them as headstrong, foolhardy, and bent on self-destruction. To many people, great effort is only worthwhile when it results in success.
>
> Adapted from Gilbert Brim, *Ambition*

Assignment: Is the effort involved in pursuing any goal valuable, even if the goal is not reached? Plan and write an essay in which you develop your point of view on this issue. Support your position with reasoning and examples taken from your reading, studies, experience, or observations.

Prompt 3

Think carefully about the issue presented in the following excerpt and the assignment below.

> Newness has become our obsession. Novelty is more interesting to us than continuing with whatever is "tried and true." We discard the old so we can acquire the most recent model, the latest version, the newest and most improved formula. Often, we replace what is useful just because it is no longer new. Not only with material goods but also with cultural values, we prefer whatever is the latest trend.

Assignment: Should people always prefer new things, ideas, or values to those of the past? Plan and write an essay in which you develop your point of view on this issue. Support your position with reasoning and examples taken from your reading, studies, experience, or observations.

Prompt 4

Think carefully about the issue presented in the following excerpt and the assignment below.

> Since we live in a global society, surely we should view ourselves as citizens of the whole world. But instead, people choose to identify and associate with smaller and more familiar groups. People think of themselves as belonging to families, nations, cultures, and generations — or as belonging to smaller groups whose members share ideas, views, or common experiences. All of these kinds of groups may offer people a feeling of security but also prevent them from learning or experiencing anything new.

Assignment: Is there any value for people to belong only to a group or groups with which they have something in common? Plan and write an essay in which you develop your point of view on this issue. Support your position with reasoning and examples taken from your reading, studies, experience, or observations.

2008 年 3 月真题作文题

Prompt 1

Think carefully about the issue presented in the following excerpt and the assignment below.

> Organizations or groups that share a common goal often mention teamwork as their secret to success by insisting that people in the group work together for the good of the entire group. However, by requiring each individual to accept the decisions of the others in the group, organizations may discourage the expression of individual talent. Ultimately, a group is most successful when all of its members are encouraged to pursue their own goals and interests.

Assignment: Are organizations or groups most successful when their members pursue individual wishes and goals? Plan and write an essay in which you develop your point of view on this issue. Support your position with reasoning and examples taken from your reading, studies, experience, or observations.

Prompt 2

Think carefully about the issue presented in the following excerpt and the assignment below.

> Being loyal-faithful or dedicated to someone or something-is not always easy. People often have conflicting loyalties, and there are no guidelines that help them decide to what or whom they should be loyal. Moreover, people are often loyal to something bad. Still, loyalty is one of the essential attributes a person must have and must demand of others.
>
> Adapted from James Carville, *Stickin': The Case for Loyalty*

Assignment: Should people always be loyal? Plan and write an essay in which you develop your point of view on this issue. Support your position with reasoning and examples taken from your reading, studies, experience, or observations.

Prompt 3

Think carefully about the issue presented in the following excerpt and the assignment below.

> Winning feels forever fabulous. But you can learn more from losing than from winning. Losing prepares you for setback and tragedy more than winning ever can. Moreover, loss invites reflection and a change of strategies. In the process of recovering from your losses, you learn how to avoid them the next time.
>
> Adapted from Pat Conroy, *My Losing Season*

Assignment: Do people learn more from losing than from winning? Plan and write an essay in which you develop your point of view on this issue. Support your position with reasoning and examples taken from your reading, studies, experience, or observations.

2008 年 5 月真题作文题

Prompt 1

Think carefully about the issue presented in the following excerpt and the assignment below.

Technological advances have freed society from tiresome labor, such as washing clothes by hand, hauling heavy loads, and walking long distances, and have given people increased access to information and entertainment. Yet, when given a choice, many people still resist using modern conveniences. There must be something to be gained from not using technology.

Assignment: Are there benefits to be gained from avoiding the use of modern technology, even when using it would make life easier? Plan and write an essay in which you develop your point of view on this issue. Support your position with reasoning and examples taken from your reading, studies, experience, or observations.

Prompt 2

Think carefully about the issue presented in the following excerpt and the assignment below.

From talent contests to the Olympics to the Nobel and Pulitzer prizes, we constantly seek to reward those who are "number one." This emphasis on recognizing the winner creates the impression that other competitors, despite working hard and well, have lost. In many cases, however, the difference between the winner and the losers is slight. The wrong person may even be selected as the winner. Awards and prizes merely distract us from valuable qualities possessed by others besides the winners.

Assignment: Do people place too much emphasis on winning? Plan and write an essay in which you develop your point of view on this issue. Support your position with reasoning and examples taken from your reading, studies, experience, or observations.

Prompt 3

Think carefully about the issue presented in the following excerpt and the assignment below.

> There are those who believe that everything we do is inspired by the desire for power in its various forms. They maintain that our actions are nothing but expressions of a striving for power. In this view, even when we act kindly toward other people, we are motivated, whether we know it or not, by a desire to have some control over their lives, for our act of kindness puts them partially in our power.
>
> Adapted from Leszek Kolakowski, _Freedom_, _Fame_, _Lying_, _and Betrayal_: _Essays on Everyday Life_

Assignment: Are people's actions motivated primarily by a desire for power over others? Plan and write an essay in which you develop your point of view on this issue. Support your position with reasoning and examples taken from your reading, studies, experience, or observations.

Prompt 4

Think carefully about the issue presented in the following excerpt and the assignment below.

> Common sense suggests an obvious division between the past and present, between history and current events. In many cases, however, this boundary is not clear cut because earlier events are not locked away in the past. Events from history remain alive through people's memories and through books, films, and other media. For both individuals and groups, incidents from the past continue to influence the present-sometimes positively and sometimes negatively.

Assignment: Do incidents from the past continue to influence the present? Plan and write an essay in which you develop your point of view on this issue. Support your position with reasoning and examples taken from your reading, studies, experience, or observations.

2008 年 6 月真题作文题

Prompt 1

Think carefully about the issue presented in the following excerpt and the assignment below.

> Most of us are convinced that fame brings happiness. Fame, it seems, is among the things people most desire. We believe that to be famous, for whatever reason, is to prove oneself and confirm that one matters in the world. And yet those who are already famous often complain of the terrible burden of fame. In fact, making the achievement of fame one's life goal involves commitments of time and effort that are usually wasted.
>
> Adapted from Leszek Kolakowski, *Freedom, Fame, Lying, and Betrayal : Essays on Everyday Life*

Assignment: Does fame bring happiness, or are people who are not famous more likely to be happy? Plan and write an essay in which you develop your point of view on this issue. Support your position with reasoning and examples taken from your reading, studies, experience, or observations.

Prompt 2

Think carefully about the issue presented in the following excerpt and the assignment below.

> A society composed of men and women who are not bound by convention-in other words, they do not act according to what others say or do-is far more lively than one in which all people behave alike. When each person's character is developed individually and differences of opinion are acceptable, it is beneficial to interact with new people because they are not mere replicas of those whom one has already met.
>
> Adapted from Bertrand Russell, *The Conquest of Happiness*

Assignment: Is it better for a society when people act as individuals rather than copying the ideas and opinions of others? Plan and write an essay in which you develop your point of view on this issue. Support your position with reasoning and examples taken from your reading, studies, experience, or observations.

Prompt 3

Think carefully about the issue presented in the following excerpt and the assignment below.

> When someone has the same ideas or views as most people do, we tend to believe that the person is reasonable and correct. Often, however, views that are considered reasonable or commonsensical are anything but sensible. Many widely held views regarding current events, science, education, arts and literature, and many other topics ultimately prove to be wrong. The fact that an idea or view is widespread — held by many people — does not make it right.

Assignment: Are widely held views often wrong, or are such views more likely to be correct? Plan and write an essay in which you develop your point of view on this issue. Support your position with reasoning and examples taken from your reading, studies, experience, or observations.

2008 年 10 月真题作文题

Prompt 1

Think carefully about the issue presented in the following excerpt and the assignment below.

> We are frequently told that compromise is the best way for people to work out their differences. When people compromise, with each side losing a little in order to reach a satisfactory agreement, both sides can continue to live in harmony. However, compromise can work only when the issues at stake are not that important. Compromise does not work when there is a genuine difference of opinion about strongly held principles or ideas.

Assignment: Is compromise always the best way to resolve a conflict? Plan and write an essay in which you develop your point of view on this issue. Support your position with reasoning and examples taken from your reading, studies, experience, or observations.

Prompt 2

Think carefully about the issue presented in the following excerpt and the assignment below.

> People usually assume that the quality of a decision is directly related to the time and effort that went into making it. We believe that we are always better off gathering as much information as possible and then spending as much time as possible analyzing that information. But there are times when making a quick judgment is the best thing to do. Decisions made quickly can be as good as decisions made slowly and cautiously.
>
> Adapted from Malcolm Gladwell, *Blink: The Power of Thinking Without Thinking*

Assignment: Are decisions made quickly just as good as decisions made slowly and

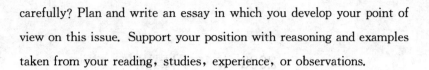

carefully? Plan and write an essay in which you develop your point of view on this issue. Support your position with reasoning and examples taken from your reading, studies, experience, or observations.

Prompt 3

Think carefully about the issue presented in the following excerpt and the assignment below.

> It is unrealistic to think that any group of people — a family, a committee, a company, a city — can function peacefully and productively without some kind of authority. The needs and interests of the individuals who make up any group are too varied for its members to operate as a unit without having someone to make the final decisions. Somebody has to be in charge; somebody has to be ultimately responsible.

Assignment: Can a group of people function effectively without someone being in charge? Plan and write an essay in which you develop your point of view on this issue. Support your position with reasoning and examples taken from your reading, studies, experience, or observations.

2008 年 11 月真题作文题

Prompt 1

Think carefully about the issue presented in the following excerpt and the assignment below.

> If an old tradition is still around today, we can assume that it deserves to remain in existence. Well-established customs, styles that are still popular, and ideas that people still find sensible survive because these traditions are strong enough to survive. Continuity guarantees quality. Old-fashioned hospitality, old-fashioned politeness, old-fashioned honor in business — all these traditions have qualities of survival. Fortunately, these will always be with us.
>
> Adapted from Jacob Braude, *Jacob Braude's Second Encyclopedia of Stories, Quotations, and Anecdotes*

Assignment: Do all established traditions deserve to remain in existence? Plan and write an essay in which you develop your point of view on this issue. Support your position with reasoning and examples taken from your reading, studies, experience, or observations.

Prompt 2

Think carefully about the issue presented in the following excerpt and the assignment below.

> We cannot appreciate what we have for its own merit. We see ourselves as fortunate only when we have as much as, or more than, other people. Thus, our judgment of what represents an appropriate limit on anything — on wealth or status or possessions — is never arrived at independently. Instead, we compare ourselves to other people, always wondering if what we have is enough.
>
> Adapted from Alain de Botton, *Status Anxiety*

Assignment: Do people need to compare themselves with others in order to appreciate what they have? Plan and write an essay in which you develop your point of view on this issue. Support your position with reasoning and examples taken from your reading, studies, experience, or observations.

Prompt 3

Think carefully about the issue presented in the following excerpt and the assignment below.

> On the surface, censorship seems objectionable because it limits our freedom. But all societies need to suppress or restrict information that is offensive or potentially harmful. People depend on the establishment of some limits, some way of making distinctions between what is right and what is wrong. Censorship is actually beneficial to a society because it helps to establish ideals of what is proper in such areas as art, music, and literature.

Assignment: Should society limit people's exposure to some kinds of information or forms of expression? Plan and write an essay in which you develop your point of view on this issue. Support your position with reasoning and examples taken from your reading, studies, experience, or observations.

Prompt 4

Think carefully about the issue presented in the following excerpt and the assignment below.

> Independent people-those who rely on themselves rather than on others-get what they want through their own efforts. Interdependent people combine their efforts with the efforts of others to achieve their goals. To be most effective, people need to be interdependent. People who do not think and act interdependently may achieve individual success, but they will not be good leaders or team players.
>
> Adapted from Stephen R. Covey, *The Seven Habits of Highly Effective People*

Assignment: Is it necessary for people to combine their efforts with those of others in order to be most effective? Plan and write an essay in which you develop your point of view on this issue. Support your position with reasoning and examples taken from your reading, studies, experience, or observations.

2008 年 12 月真题作文题

Prompt 1

Think carefully about the issue presented in the following excerpt and the assignment below.

> The biggest difference between people who succeed at any difficult undertaking and those who do not is not ability but persistence. Many extremely talented people give up when obstacles arise. After all, who wants to face failure? It is often said about highly successful people that they are just ordinary individuals who kept on trying, who did not give up.
>
> Adapted from Tom Morris, *True Success: A New Philosophy of Excellence*

Assignment: Is persistence more important than ability in determining a person's success? Plan and write an essay in which you develop your point of view on this issue. Support your position with reasoning and examples taken from your reading, studies, experience, or observations.

Prompt 2

Think carefully about the issue presented in the following excerpt and the assignment below.

> Whether it is a child pouting to get ice cream or a politician using emotionally charged language to influence potential supporters, all people use some form of acting to achieve whatever ends they seek. Public figures of all kinds would have short, unsuccessful careers without the aid of acting. Acting — consciously assuming a role in order to achieve some purpose — is a tool people use to protect their interests and gain advantages in every aspect of life.
>
> Adapted from Marlon Brando, *Foreword to The Technique of Acting by Stella Adler*

Assignment: Is acting an essential part of everyday life? Plan and write an essay in which you develop your point of view on this issue. Support your position with reasoning and examples taken from your reading, studies, experience, or observations.

Prompt 3

Think carefully about the issue presented in the following excerpt and the assignment below.

When people are very enthusiastic — always willing and eager to meet new challenges or give undivided support to ideas or projects — they are likely to be rewarded. They often work harder and enjoy their work more than do those who are more restrained. But there are limits to how enthusiastic people should be. People should always question and doubt, since too much enthusiasm can prevent people from considering better ideas, goals, or courses of action.

Assignment: Can people have too much enthusiasm? Plan and write an essay in which you develop your point of view on this issue. Support your position with reasoning and examples taken from your reading, studies, experience, or observations.

2009 年 1 月真题作文题

Prompt 1

Think carefully about the issue presented in the following excerpt and the assignment below.

> Planning lets people impose order on the chaotic processes of making or doing something new. Too much planning, however, can lead people to follow the same predetermined course of action, to do things the same way they were done before. Creative thinking is about breaking free from the way that things have always been. That is why it is vital for people to know the difference between good planning and too much planning.
>
> Adapted from Twyla Tharp, *The Creative Habit*

Assignment: Does planning interfere with creativity? Plan and write an essay in which you develop your point of view on this issue. Support your position with reasoning and examples taken from your reading, studies, experience, or observations.

Prompt 2

Think carefully about the issue presented in the following excerpt and the assignment below.

> Most people underestimate their own abilities. They tend to remember their failures more vividly than their successes, and for this reason they have unrealistically low expectations about what they are capable of. Those individuals who distinguish themselves through great accomplishments are usually no more talented than the average person: they simply set higher standards for themselves, since they have higher expectations about what they can do.

Assignment: Do highly accomplished people achieve more than others mainly because they expect more of themselves? Plan and write an essay in which you develop your point of view on this issue. Support your position with reasoning and examples taken from your reading, studies, experience, or observations.

Prompt 3

Think carefully about the issue presented in the following excerpt and the assignment below.

> People are taught that they should not go back on their decisions. In fact, our society supports the notion that to change your mind is evidence of weakness and unreliability, leading many people to say, "Once I decide, I decide!" But why do people make such a statement? If factors, feelings, and ideas change, isn't the ability to make a new decision evidence of flexibility, adaptability, and strength?
>
> Adapted from Theodore I. Rubin, *Compassion and Self-Hate*

Assignment: Should people change their decisions when circumstances change, or is it best for them to stick with their original decisions? Plan and write an essay in which you develop your point of view on this issue. Support your position with reasoning and examples taken from your reading, studies, experience, or observations.

2009 年 3 月真题作文题

Prompt 1

Think carefully about the issue presented in the following excerpt and the assignment below.

> Many people believe that being honest and honorable limits their options, their opportunities, their very ability to succeed. Unfortunately, in today's me-first culture, ethics may be the *only* thing people choose to live without! They believe they have only two choices: (1) to win by doing whatever it takes, even if it is wrong, or (2) to be ethical and therefore lose. Few people set out to be dishonest, but nobody wants to lose.
>
> Adapted from John C. Maxwell, *There's No Such Thing as "Business" Ethics*

Assignment: Does being ethical make it hard to be successful? Plan and write an essay in which you develop your point of view on this issue. Support your position with reasoning and examples taken from your reading, studies, experience, or observations

Prompt 2

Think carefully about the issue presented in the following excerpt and the assignment below.

> Whatever happened to good manners? Many books and articles have been written about the lack of common courtesy and old-fashioned politeness in today's society. From spoiled children acting out in restaurants to so-called experts yelling at each other on cable news shows, people seem less concerned with good manners and civilized behavior than ever before. On the other hand, if people really want to change the world for the better, they have to risk being seen as impolite or uncivil.

Assignment: Is it sometimes necessary to be impolite? Plan and write an essay in which you develop your point of view on this issue. Support your position with reasoning and examples taken from your reading, studies, experience, or observations.

Prompt 3

Think carefully about the issue presented in the following excerpt and the assignment below.

> We define "courage" too loosely. Real courage is conscious self-sacrifice, either for the sake of others or to uphold a value. But we typically identify a single aspect of courage — daring or honesty, for example — as the entire virtue. We even say it takes courage to differ from the mainstream in one's preferences in fashion or music or to speak out about certain wrongs. Such acts, though admirable, are not necessarily courageous.
>
> Adapted from John McCain with Mark Salter, *Why Courage Matters*

Assignment: Should we limit our use of the term "courage" to acts in which people risk their own well-being for the sake of others or to uphold a value? Plan and write an essay in which you develop your point of view on this issue. Support your position with reasoning and examples taken from your reading, studies, experience, or observations.

图书在版编目（CIP）数据

SAT 作文/张一冰编著 . —上海：上海译文出版社，
2009.12 （2012.10 重印）
（美国高校入学考试指导丛书）
ISBN 978 - 7 - 5327 - 4831 - 0

Ⅰ. S⋯ Ⅱ. 张⋯ Ⅲ. 英语—写作—高等学校—入学考
试—美国—自学参考资料 Ⅳ. H315

中国版本图书馆 CIP 数据核字（2009）第 080849 号

SAT 作文
——美国高校入学考试指导丛书

张一冰　编著

上海世纪出版股份有限公司
译文出版社出版
网址：www.yiwen.com.cn
上海世纪出版股份有限公司发行中心发行
200001　上海福建中路 193 号　www.ewen.cc
上海市印刷七厂有限公司印刷

开本 787×1092　1/16　印张 14.25　字数 253,000
2009 年 12 月第 1 版　2012 年 10 月第 4 次印刷
印数：12,401–15,600 册
ISBN 978 - 7 - 5327 - 4831 - 0/H · 900
定价：31.00 元

如有质量问题，请与承印厂质量科联系。T：021 - 69113557